THE WEALTH

HOW TO GO FROM MIDDLE CLASS TO WEALTHY

CREATION FORMULA

NEW YORK TIMES BESTSELLING AUTHOR

GRANT CARDONE

The Wealth Creation Formula

Published by Cardone Training Technologies, Inc.
18909 NE 29th Avenue Aventura,
FL 33180
310-777-0255

Visit our website at www.GrantCardone.com
Printed in the United States of America

First Edition Printed: 2023
ISBN: 979-8-218-28982-9

CONTENTS

INTRODUCTION

NOT-SO 'SHOCKING'

When you go after a core societal belief the way I'm about to, you're supposed to kick things off with a "shocking" opener — especially when it's something as deeply ingrained as "The Middle-Class American Dream."

Typically, it might probably sound something like: "The American Dream is Dead!" or "The middle class is a hoax." But those two statements aren't really shocking at all, are they? Anyone who's been alive the past three or four generations already knows they're both at least partially true. The main issue is that there hasn't been a replacement solution for the idea of the "Middle-Class American Dream", so, by default, most people cling to this shared delusion.

All that said, let me deliver my "shocking" opener for you: the middle class is far worse than "dead" or just a "hoax". It's actually our society's current "slave" class. And, if you're someone who's bought into the hoax, I'm sorry to tell you this, but you are a SLAVE. So, my goal in this book is to put you on the path to "middle-class emancipation".

The middle-income trap is defined as: *"an economic development situation in which a country that attains a certain income (due to given advantages) gets stuck at that level."*

Sound familiar?

Most Americans today are barely living paycheck to paycheck, or worse, they're using debt to get by. Why? Because of a massive financial brainwashing operation in America. It's gone on for decades now. The "rules" that most people work, save and invest by are not the real rules of creating wealth in America. No. They're the house rules, created by those who get rich while you stay stuck and poor. It's not your fault. As you'll see, it's what "they" have trained you to do.

But there's good news. There are rules you can follow to become wealthy. You can have it all. You just need to run the right financial program in your life. That's why I wrote the "Wealth Creation Formula." I'm going to give you the formula to becoming wealthy in America today.

Consider this book your wealth creation plan where I'll unpack the 9 traps that the media, the "man" and the misinformed have perpetuated to keep you trapped and clinging to the narrative they continue to push. And then, I'll show you the exact formula for creating wealth. These common traps may surprise you, like someone telling you that the Earth is flat, but don't disregard this information without researching it more. Read on and arrive at your own conclusions, based on the personal stories and the evidence I'm about to present. Don't be part of the masses who financially imprison themselves. Commit to creating wealth for you, your family and your community.

And if you're currently stuck striving in the middle class right now, don't feel too bad about it. Up until today, you've had a pass, because it's not really anything you had a formula for escaping and creating prosperity. But as of today, you will have an alternative solution for creating wealth. And by choosing to read this book any further, you've reached a "fork" in the road of your awareness.

So, if you continue reading past this point, you're admitting that you want my help. You want the formula for getting rich in America today. To get untrapped and step into a much better and more powerful way of living. If you let me, I can and will help you. I understand that, just like my own parents, while they were still here, you may not yet realize that there is an escape route — another path you can and should be on.

This book's 9-step formula is the blueprint to escaping the three kinds of traps the middle class is built on, plus creating indestructible wealth that will provide for you and your loved ones for generations. The three kinds of traps most Americans are stuck in are:

1. **Money traps**
2. **Education traps**
3. **Asset traps**

Money traps are things related to your job; how you think about saving and how you handle using credit cards.

Education traps are about all the things we learn from the "man" (the government and educational institutions), the media and the misinformed (the people around us who've been brainwashed into believing the middle class still exists).

Asset traps are about the millions of people who are investing in illusions. So many people "save for retirement" for decades, hoping their money will return, multiplied. Most will soon find out they do not have enough money to support themselves after they retire. The reality is, the money that was taken out of their paychecks got diversified toward illusions, making the rich richer, with their necks left on the chopping block.

The Wealth Creation Formula is the exact 9 steps to get you out of these traps and on the path to prosperity. It is the rule set for going from poor or middle class to wealthy.

I've broken everything up into four manageable sections, each made up of straight-shooting chapters. The first three sections explain the "money", "education" and "asset" traps. I'll show you how to spot and avoid the ones you may not have fallen into yet. Then, in Section 4, I'll lay out The Wealth Creation Formula — exactly how to escape any trap you may currently find yourself caught in. Some of these include the flawed concept of "home ownership"; the big "a college degree is a must" lie; and the hopelessly false idea that "retirement is a never-ending vacation".

And make no mistake about it, this is not some feel good book or one of those dusty lectures full of outdated "theories". This is the most current and practical information you can get. It will change everything you think, and every action you take, regarding wealth creation. It's time to throw off your middle-class shackles and kick the habit of smoking the pipe of the long dead "American Dream".

Fair warning though: If you're someone who's not as familiar with me and my approach yet, this book will be brutally honest. I'm about to tear down the facade of middle-class mediocrity that's been driven so deeply into our core. And show you the true formula for creating wealth in America. The trade-off for the pain of my brutal honesty is that today is the day you get to kick the middle-class habit and start achieving your most powerful dreams.

It's my goal with this book to wake you and millions of other people up. Imagine if just 10% of the people currently stuck in the middle-class trap learned to escape its clutches, hitting new levels of success previously perceived as "impossible"?

Defying convention is my stock-in-trade, so if you're ready to follow my formula, create true lasting wealth for sure and kick the middle-class habit and change your own future and the world, then read on. But no matter what, I can promise you one thing. You'll never again think the same way about wealth and the "American Dream", because after today, you'll be too focused on turning your own dream into reality.

DADDY, WHAT'S THE MIDDLE CLASS?

I was once delivering a live stream to just shy of 20,000 people. The topic was mistakes I made that cost me millions of dollars. Out of nowhere, my then 6-year-old daughter Sabrina suddenly walked in (as she's known to do). She'd heard me say the word "middle class" as I was talking and jumped in (as she's also known to do).

Her question was, "What's the middle class?" A great question from someone unafraid to ask it. You've probably heard the term "middle class" thousands of times, especially from politicians using it to try and hustle your vote. So, let me talk about what it practically means, as opposed to what it actually means.

Different websites will give you different income numbers for what can be defined as the "middle class", but let's keep things simple. It's not rocket science. The term "middle class" is technically defined as a household that earns between $40,000 and $115,000 yearly. So, in many areas of the country, you're considered right in the center of the middle class if your household is within that range.

When I explained it to Sabrina, I was thinking about how I always wanted money at her age. See, before my dad died, when I was ten years old, he wasn't able to spend much time with me. The guy was under tremendous amounts of stress and pressure, living the middle-class "dream", when it was still actually kind of possible. That meant taking care of his family; five kids and a wife, as he built himself into the middle class.

So, when I was trying to explain it to her, I said, "'middle class' means right in the middle of things. There's one group of people over here — they're poor. Then, there's another group of people over there — they're rich. And then there are these people in the middle."

Her response was so profound, I can't imagine anyone being able to explain it any better than she did. With the kind of wisdom that only a 6-year-old has, she asked, "So, the middle class are rich people who are poor?" I couldn't help exclaiming, "Exactly right, Sabrina! That's exactly right!"

So, if you're someone who makes more than people you consider poor, but you're way behind people you consider "rich", then you're self-described middle class. This may even include things like, providing a college education for your kids and a 401(k)!

And, if you don't live in the ghetto, but your house sits far from the gates of whatever the "Beverly Hills" is of the place you live in, then you're likely middle class. Not concentrating on what you make or what you have, the middle class is really just a shorthand way of saying that you're a poor, rich person. If you have any thought that getting rich is unnecessary, that you just want to be happy and money won't make you happy, then you have a middle-class mindset.

That one flawed way of thinking is what this book is really about. I'm writing this to cure you of that God awful misinformed middle-class mindset, once and forever. And show you the real formula for how true wealth is created.

WHY DON'T POLITICIANS TALK ABOUT WEALTH?

Did you ever notice that politicians don't talk about Americans creating wealth? Instead, they talk more about the middle class. And they talk about the middle class more than anyone else. That's the dead giveaway that the middle class is a lie. And have also noticed that the more they talk about the middle class, the worse it gets for most Americans? They're always saying, "We need to save the Middle Class!", even though they know it really doesn't exist anymore.

If you were brought up like me, as part of the "poor middle class", you were taught not to like money. My mom used to remind us all the time that we weren't poor. She regularly said things like, "Look, you've got a bicycle, you've got electricity, you've got air conditioning. You have way more than I had, so be grateful."

Have you ever heard that and the pitch that goes with it: "If you just get in the middle class, get a good house, get a good education, get married, have a couple kids, everything will be great!" If you have, you were raised to aim for the middle class. You never talked about being "wealthy" let alone how to become wealthy.

That's why you're in the situation you're in today. If you are brought up with poor middle-class thinking, you inherit the ideas of the poor in the middle class. And those ideas don't work anymore. In America today, what used to be the bulging middle class is mostly just bulging into poverty. There are really only two groups in America that are growing right now: the "poor" class and the "rich" class. That should tell you everything you need to know about the state of the middle class.

Here's what they didn't teach you in school about becoming wealthy instead of just surviving the middle class. It takes money. It takes lots and lots of money. The reality in America is that we've been sold a bill of goods that because we're in America, we're better, simply because we're "free".

But the truth is, even if people in the country are free, they're not independent. I mean *financially* independent. We live on an economic planet. You can be free and poor. But to be independent, you need money. This is the good news and the bad news. According to a recent LendingClub report 61% of Americans live paycheck to paycheck in the richest country on the planet, and they make sense of it because they're not in India. The only difference is the village. This "USA" village has big buildings and the "India" village doesn't. Is there any other real difference though when you're still living paycheck to paycheck, stuck in the middle-class trap?

One big catalyst that led to me developing my Wealth Creation Formula, the core of the middle-class escape plan, was being at a charity event. There were 250 middle-class people in attendance. I walked out of the event, realizing how many of them wanted to escape the middle class, not to have more so they can buy another toy, trip or house. They just wanted to create wealth, so they'd have enough money to give more of it away.

The problem that night was that most of those attendees were stuck in the middle class. They didn't have the formula I'm going to give you. They wanted to help hit the $2 million target at the charity event that night, but only a handful of them could actually give money to make it happen.

So, I came home that night, after having a conversation with my wife, motivated to help people who want more, not just material possessions or for themselves. I'm driven to find ways to help people who want to have more in order to take care of their church, charity and community.

Following The Wealth Creation Formula will put you on the path to go from wherever you are right now, to true wealth and the peace of mind that comes with it. It's the only position where you can truly control your life and protect the health and well-being of the people you care about, your spouse, your family, your extended family and of course you, yourself — whoever you feel it's your job to be there for.

Section One: "MONEY" TRAPS

Section Summary: In this first section you'll get clear on the three biggest "money" traps keeping you from creating wealth.

I. **The "Job Hate" Trap**
Where thinking the wrong way about your job as the stepping stone it actually is, leaves you feeling stuck and ultimately trapped in it, only because you believe you are.

II. **The "Piggy Bank" Trap**
Where saving money for the wrong reasons keeps you from ever doing anything that leads to real wealth.

III. **The "Plastic" Trap**
The trap that keeps you reliant on credit cards, because you don't understand how you can use them as oil, instead of sand inside your financial engine.

If you haven't fallen into any of these traps yet, this section will help you steer clear of them. And, if you have, I'll set you up to escape them!

I.
The "Job Hate" Trap

You'll find out how working a job can be a middle-class trap, but only if you fail to use it as a stepping stone to break the cycle and leverage the Wealth Creation Formula. There are three important points to pay attention to:

1. **The <u>only</u> two income classes** (hint: "middle class" ain't one!)

2. **The path from a "job" to "rich", then ultimately "wealthy"** (there IS a difference between rich and wealthy)

3. **Developing an insane work ethic** (even if people have called you "lazy" or "unfocused" your whole life)

BE RICH OR BE LEFT BEHIND

The date, February 1, 2015. The time, less than 90 minutes after Super Bowl XLIX had ended. The deafening crowd had barely cleared out of the University of Phoenix Stadium in Glendale, Arizona. Tom Brady, the winning quarterback, was showered, packed and dressed, headed back from the game to his hotel. That's when the text came in from his long-time friend, John Falk, "Congratulations buddy. What's next?"

Tom's response can only be described as the definition of work ethic: "Thinking about how to get ring number five." He had just won his fourth Super Bowl. Was he thinking about champagne or Disneyland? No. Tom's mind was already on the work required to get his fifth ring. That's the type of man Tom Brady is. His mind is always on the work he's got to put in to complete the job at hand. And when the job is done? Then, he gets right back to work. Likewise, you've got to understand the role of your job. Specifically, what's the role of your job when it comes to escaping the middle-class trap and creating wealth?

In February 2023, Tom Brady announced his retirement marking the end of an illustrious career that saw him achieve unparalleled success. With an astonishing seven Super Bowl victories to his name, Brady's remarkable leadership, skill, and determination have solidified his legacy as one of the greatest athletes in sports history.

We'll start with the basics. There are only three income classes. You're either wealthy, you're rich or you're poor — and to me, poor means you're being left behind. My definition of wealthy is when you have an abundance of things that are valuable including money that's making you more money. "Rich" means having a lot of money and maybe material possessions, and it's a step toward "wealthy". "Poor" is when you're making just enough to pay your bills, with maybe a little left over, but you're not getting ahead. There are seven signs that you're being left behind.

NOTE: If at least three of these are true for you, you're left behind right now. Read on and I'll show you how to change that.

The 7 Warnings Signs You're Being Left Behind:

1. **Earning Less Than 3x Expenses:** Not earning at least three times as much each month as your monthly expenses
2. **Plastic for Bills:** Needing to use credit cards to pay monthly bills
3. **"Wish" Instead of "Will":** Using phrases like "I want" or I wish" instead of "When I" and "I will"
4. **No Passive Income:** You don't have multiple streams of income, including passive income streams
5. **Less Than Three Months:** Unable to survive for more than three months if your source of income got lost
6. **Middle-Class Comfort Zone:** Complacency that convinces you that more money won't make you happy and you don't really want more than you already have

7. **Viewing a Paper Degree as "Necessary":** Believing a college degree is required for financial success

It doesn't matter if you're making a hundred thousand or even half a million a year. If your money isn't making you serious money — you are being left behind! All those poor souls stuck in the middle class focus on working a job just to pay their bills. They're not committed to working as a stepping stone to getting wealthy. Why? Because somebody told them, "You can't change your condition." But that's not true. All you've got to do is ask yourself, "Who has changed their financial condition in my community and how did they do it?"

Who's someone who has broken out of an area like Baltimore or Detroit, someone who's not a musician or an athlete. Show me someone who's transcended a rural or suburban area, someone without a scholarship, a trust fund or any super talents. Look for someone who made it out without getting "lucky". Figure out who you should model and follow. They're probably not on Instagram. They're probably too busy running a business. Figure out how to get connected with those people and figure out how they did it. I'll dive deeper into this in The "Millionaire Next Door" Trap.

The most important thing to understand is that your focus has got to be on the commitment to getting out of wherever you are unless you think you're fine. But if you feel stuck, then you're being left behind, regardless of where you are. You could be in the middle class, with country club memberships and two BMWs.

I know people that are paying so much interest for their homes, their cars, their country clubs and their kids' tuition that are actually poorer than people who earn very little. Someone I know paid $350,000 to send his daughter to school. Now she works at Whole Foods. Does that sound like getting ahead to you? I'll share more of this story in The "Higher Education" Trap.

To financially feed the institutions on this planet it takes more than just the backs of people "technically" categorized as poor. It takes a lot of middle class backs as well. Most of the $1.7 trillion of college debt, for example, is on the backs of the middle class. Tuition borrowers from households in the middle class owe on average $43 090 in student loan debt. They account for more than 65% of the nation's outstanding student loan debt.

If you don't learn how to earn passive income, you're going to spend your whole life working just to pay the bills. At the time of this death, Edgar Bronfman Sr., the owner of Seagrams, had a net worth of $2.6 billion. He said, "To turn $100 into $110 is work. To turn $100 million into $110 million is inevitable."

But what do people in the left-behind class do with their money? They put it in the bank. They open a checking account or savings account to store their money there until they can send it off to Wall Street. And if you're reading this, you've got to decide for yourself, right now, that you're going to break the cycle, get out of the trap and start creating wealth. You have to get out of harm's way or the system will run you over. Make a decision that you're going to break the cycle starting here and now.

This book won't break it for everybody, because only a small group of the people who read it will take advantage of it. 99% will critique it, hate on it, judge it, or point out where they think I'm wrong. Less than 1% will say, "Hey, I gotta wake up. I gotta change what I'm doing. I gotta start paying attention to my money."

Since you're still here, past that fork in the road I mentioned in the intro, there's hope for you. The choice is simple though: Be in that 1% that's open to the advice I'm giving here about the three money traps and get into the "rich" class or stay in that 99% and be left behind.

You have to figure out what you're going to do, to not only protect your money, but grow it. Initially your cash flow is going to probably come from the job you're maybe feeling trapped by and hating right now. For now, the money you're earning is yours (at least temporarily), so where can you go to start earning 5% or 6% percent per year on it?

As part of the Wealth Creation Formula, which I'll show you in the following chapters, I'll show you how to keep your eyes open to opportunities that will return you 8%, 10% even 15% and higher. But don't worry about that right now. Just understand that your job doesn't NEED to feel like a dead end, when it's really just the FRONT DOOR to creating wealth and escaping the middle-class trap.

COWBOY WISDOM

When it comes to having a job, be sure you're clear about one thing: Your job only becomes a trap when you stay stuck in it. Otherwise, it's a stepping stone along your journey from the middle class to rich.

Pretty much everyone understands the principle of needing to practice something they might feel like they hate in order to succeed. As a player in the NBA, Michael Jordan for example, would spend the first hour of his daily warm-up, every day, working out overlooked-yet-vital areas like his wrists, fingers, ankles and toes. It takes commitment and discipline to do something that mundane. If Air Jordan needs to do it, so do you. Quitting a job because you don't like some parts of it will only send you to another job you hate.

> *"Labor gives birth to ideas."*
> ~Jim Rohn

> *"I have been up against tough competition all my life. I wouldn't know how to get along without it."*
> ~Walt Disney

"The idea of having a steady job is appealing."
~Robin Williams

"Nothing will work unless you do."
~Maya Angelou

"Wherever you go, there you are."
~"Cowboy"

That last quote comes from my old friend, "Cowboy". He used to always say, "Wherever you go, there you are." And that's always stuck with me because it's so true. Wherever I go, I can get rid of my girlfriend, I can get a different job or a new car, but I'm still there — me and all my limitations and my problems.

I got fired from six jobs — that's every job I ever had. Even McDonald's fired me, and it's not easy to get fired from McDonald's. I totally deserved it though because I was terrible as an employee. I hated it and I had a bad attitude about it. I was resentful instead of being grateful for it. The plain truth is, I didn't understand why anybody would work there.

Next, I got fired from the country club as a busboy. I couldn't even make waiter. It pissed me off because I would set the table and people wouldn't even acknowledge my existence, let alone thank me or anything. Nobody even looked at me and it killed me — like I was nothing.

Then I lost a job at a refinery. That was hard labor. I lost that job after only three months. After that, I worked on a fishing boat, then in a furniture store, where I was trying to sell furniture with a bunch of women — tough competition. Then I was a clothing salesman, but not for long! That's six jobs where I got the hatchet. The last job I had was as a car salesman. I ended up getting fired from that same job too — six times! But I refused to leave, because I was good at it and it paid well, which is the point I'm making here.

You have to find a job that pays you enough to get at least a little bit ahead. And then, even if you hate it, you need to have enough faith in yourself to keep at it until you've got things in place where your money is making more money. That's the trick.

Me, I could definitely sling a car! I sold a lot of them. I ended up in the top 1% in the country. Every day I'd show up to work an hour and a half early and stay till midnight. Everybody else would go home, but me, I'd stay there, hunting, sniffing, on the phone, pounding. It's where I really started what I consider to be my career. But I had a college education, so I thought to myself, "What am I doing selling cars? I'm supposed to be an accountant." It was a conflict for me, because deep down I felt like I was "better" than that kind of a job. No one was hiring accountants at that time though. So, there I was with a good paying job, sabotaging it at every turn.

They used to call me "Crash", because every few months, I'd wreck a car, usually driving while high. And every time I crashed one, I'd get fired. And I'd freak out wondering to myself, "What am I going to do?" Then I'd solve the problem the same way every time I got fired. I'd crash a car and, Rip, the owner would tell me, "That's it, son, you're done! Pack your stuff up and get out of here!", and I'd immediately go find a customer and sell them. Then I'd bring him the deal and say, "Look Rip, I know you fired me and I'm done here, but I got a deal. You want to sign off on this one before I go?", and of course a car dealer is going to take the deal! Six times he fired me, and six times I got back in.

So, you start your journey from the middle class to rich by finding whatever pays you the most and instead of hating it or resenting it, you find a way to love it. Because the best way to move from the middle class to rich is with a j-o-b. It's not the worst way to get rich, like so many online say. It's step #1 to getting rich, unless you've got some mutant level talent or a daddy with a trust fund. And if you're like most people, you probably don't have either of those.

Everyone who's ever accumulated wealth started with a damn job!

I challenge you to give me one example of real success where my post above is not the case. Every one of the people you know who have moved from poor to rich to wealthy had a job first. Steve Jobs did. Elon Musk did. Bill Gates did.

For six years I was a car salesman, and even though I felt like I hated it, I became great at it — one of the best. My approach was making a commitment to embrace the thing that meant the most in that position — production. I made up my mind to go ahead and do what was in front of me, to figure out how to talk to people.

First, I learned how to handle one person at a time. If you gave me more than one person though, let's say a married couple, it freaked me out. I could not handle two people. Then I made up my mind to discipline myself to learn the art of handling both the husband and the wife, because it is just part of the job.

After that, if there were three or four people, that would freak me out. I thought, "There's no way I can sell four people," and I would hate any situation where there was more than two people because they would mess up my deal.

The kids were the worst. They'd say stuff like, "The back is too small.", and I'd think, "Shut up. I'm selling cars here kid. I don't need that from you, son!" I'd waste time and energy getting frustrated and angry.

Then, I re-upped and decided again to just master what was required to hit the next level for that job. And as I started believing in the back of my mind that there was a light at the end of the tunnel, I realized that something. That job was my best chance to break free of the cycle. This was my ticket to escape the middle-class trap that had ensnared my parents.

YOU CAN GET RICH FROM YOUR JOB

In order to purchase my middle-class emancipation ticket, I originally just kept stashing cash, so I could buy my first real estate deal. In the end though, I could have made things happen a lot faster. I just needed to realize one truth about getting my money making me more money sooner. I call it the "lots of doors" rule.

"NEVER DEPEND ON ONE OF ANYTHING — NOT EVER."

For anything you do to really succeed, you need a lot of "doors". For example, one of the biggest reasons Amazon works is because they've got a lot of doors into their platform.

A lot of people act like everybody makes money on real estate, but that's not true. Millions of families across the country lost their homes from 2008 to 2010. It wasn't a handful of people, and they didn't just lose their house and the profits — they lost their credit. I made a similar mistake. It cost me three years on my first real estate deal. I used the money I'd been stashing from my car sales job to buy my first property, but I got too attached to it. What I should have done was get into that deal, put a tenant in it and sell the house to somebody else who would collect the rent. I held onto it though because I didn't understand how the marketplace really operates.

All that said, it was the job I thought I "hated" that ultimately saved me. See, I kept it and I spent the next three years in Houston shopping real estate deals. I stayed focused on learning what the big real estate moguls do. I'm talking about people like the late Sam Zell or Fred Trump, Donald Trump's father. They always bought multiple doors and rented them out, typically in one location. That way they had big cash flows that weren't dependent on one "door".

My next real estate purchase was a $1.9 million, 38-unit complex in San Diego. I put $350,000 down on a large unit. I was only able to do that because I'd been banking cash for three years in the same essential job role.

I got really good at the auto sales space, so people knew about me. That led me to start consulting manufacturers around the United States. I would take all the extra money and just stash it off to the side. I didn't understand stocks. I didn't want to trade paper for paper. I wanted to be in metal, glass and concrete — something I could touch.

It took me three years. I constantly researched deals to get comfortable enough to know the right one to pull the trigger on. And that j-o-b I hated was the key to that.

BEATING THE SUN UP

Once you realize the truth about the role a job actually fills in your climb up from roadkill to wealthy, something suddenly happens. Your work ethic becomes something other people just can't compete with. You become untouchable.

There's no magic formula for developing a strong work ethic. I went from getting fired from every job I had, to being in the top 1% in the country at it. The real key is understanding the role that a job holds along your journey from left behind to rich and using that awareness to build a work ethic where you're beating the sun up every day and loving it. You'll never feel bad because you beat the sun up. Early in the day, you may be dragging butt, but by the end of the day you're going to be like, "Man, I'm sure glad I did this today. This was awesome!"

There's just something that happens before sun comes up that's special. It's just a different part of the day. It makes you feel good about yourself. I see so many people get sucked into their own victories. And, because their work ethic is broken, they don't keep working. They pat themselves on the back, "I got my deal, now it's time for a vacation." And you see the destruction of these people.

Just like when Tom Brady won the Super Bowl, he was immediately preparing for the next one. The work ethic of anyone I know at the top is so prevalent. And it's about more than just you. Your work ethic is contagious. You start pushing whoever you're working with and whoever you're in friendly competition with. Work ethic has no budget. You can't go broke on it. It's never going to be bad for you.

The mistake too many people make is moving too quickly away from that job they think they hate. And that is a trap in and of itself. There's this idea that you're going to be a solopreneur and outsource everything, working just four hours a week. People like me and you work hard and need motivation. The idea of the "4-hour per week, laptop lifestyle" is complete B.S. You cannot outsource everything. Remember that your job is your first stepping stone from middle class to rich to wealthy.

Stick around through Section 4. I'm going to unpack this idea as part of implementing The Wealth Creation Formula. I'll show you exactly how to use your job as the stepping stone it needs to be, instead of seeing it as something you should hate.

THE "JOB HATE" TRAP ASSESSMENT QUESTIONS:

1. **Circle the one that <u>most</u> applies: Do you consider yourself:**
   - A. Poor (5)
   - B. Lower "middle class" (4)
   - C. Mid "middle class" (3)
   - D. Upper "middle class" (2)
   - E. Wealthy (1)

2. **Which of the "Left Behind Red Flags" are true for you?**
   - ☐ Earning Less Than 3X Expenses (1)
   - ☐ Plastic for Bills (1)
   - ☐ "Wish" Instead of "Will" (1)
   - ☐ No Passive Income (1)
   - ☐ Less Than Three Months (1)
   - ☐ Middle-Class Comfort Zone (1)
   - ☐ Viewing a Paper Degree as "Necessary" (1)

3. **How capable do you currently believe you are to move from left behind to wealthy?**
   - A. Not capable (3)
   - B. Slightly capable (2)
   - C. Very capable (Grant, give me my wealth creation plan!) (1)

4. **How do you feel about your current job?**
   - A. Hate it (3)
   - B. Means to an end (2)
   - C. Love it (1)

5. **What is your annual income?**
   - A. Less than $50,000 (4)
   - B. Between $50,000-$80,000 (3)
   - C. Between $80,000-$150,000 (2)
   - D. More than $150,000 (1)

6. How would you rate your work ethic?

A. Great (1)
B. Okay (2)
C. Bad (3)

TOTAL SCORE:

* *These scores will be addressed in Section Four: The Wealth Creation Formula.*

II. The "Piggy Bank" Trap

You're about to find out how to think about what money really is, to help you start making more of it fast, including:

1. **Where the middle-class hustle really is** (hint: the banks are running it on you)

2. **Why cash is trash and cash flow is the king, the queen, the jack and the ace!**

3. **The difference between "earned" and "investment" income**

A PENNY BURNED

Have you ever heard the story of the twin brothers who ended up in two extremely different places in life? One became wildly wealthy and the other died stressed out and broke. On his deathbed, at age 65, the broke brother was asked by his son, "Dad, why did you end up so stressed out and poor?" With his final breath, he told his son, "Your grandmother told me to save all the money I made. In the end the money lost its value, and I just couldn't keep up as I got older. I'm sorry son."

On his deathbed at the ripe old age of 90, the wealthy twin's son asked him the same question. With a smile on his face as he was passing away, he said, "Your grandmother told me to save all the money I made." So, I did. Your grandfather told me to invest the money I'd saved in things that create cash flow. So, I did. In the end, I always had more money coming in than going out, so there was no way to become anything other than wealthy." With that, he died — a smile on his face.

THE 1ST RULE OF MONEY:
MONEY IS ONLY VALUABLE WHEN IT GETS USED

Let's talk about the 5-letter word that's near and dear to pretty much everybody's heart, m-o-n-e-y. I want to paint a vivid picture for you by getting you to imagine burning money... literally. There will be fire and gasoline used in the analogy I'm about to make, so keep yourself at a safe distance. Oh, and wear a warm winter jacket.

And, by the way, I'm not using this money-burning analogy for impact only. I want you to think about what the real reasons are that you probably don't have as much money as you might want; why you've struggled with it; and why I also struggled with it for so many years.

First, let me share three things that no one ever taught me about money. These three small things will change everything for you when it comes to the way you think about what it really is, how you use it, spend it and invest it. And to set all this up the right way, let's talk about the big question that really needs to be asked and answered. Who decides what money is worth, how and why?

To help make it clear what I'm getting at, go ahead and imagine two stacks of crisp, 100-dollar bills. Visualize me holding one stack in my right hand that's three inches high, so about 750 bills total. And then, directly next to me, on my left, imagine a 10-foot cube — about 200,000 bills in total. If I ask you, which of the two stacks you'd rather have, so which is more valuable, you (and anyone with any basic sense) would say the 10-foot cube, right?

Why would you say that though? I mean, what's your answer based on? If it's based on the belief that both stacks were printed at the Treasury Department's Bureau of Engraving and Printing, you'd be wrong. Because, on closer inspection, you'll see that the 10-foot cube was printed by a novelty company — let's call it the Acme Co. — the source of all Wile E. Coyote's props from the old Looney Tunes, Road Runner flicks.

"Cash is useless unless it's used.
Make it work for you."

Once I revealed the fact that the 10-foot pile was ordered from Acme Co., your opinion about the value of these hypothetical bills is going to change, isn't it? I mean, you've only got 750 "real" bills, but they've got Franklin's face on them and legit serial numbers. What are they worth — $7,500? According to common thinking, the "real" bills are worth way more than novelty bills, aren't they?

So, again, my question is, "Why?" Who determines what they're worth?" In my opinion, the real value of either stack of bills is how they get put to use. In this case, their value is as a prop, to demonstrate an important point to you. Both piles are essentially produced the same way, using a printer. And yet, once you become aware that the 10-foot stack is from Acme Novelty Co., not the BEP you quite naturally give the three-inch stack more value, right?

But let me take this analogy one step further. Let's say you and I are in the Alaskan wilderness during the dead of winter, with these same two stacks of bills. I've dropped you off at a cabin in the middle of nowhere — no phone, no Internet, no means of travel. I tell you I'll be leaving you in the cabin for two weeks. You have to survive through sub-zero weather. All you've got other than whichever stack of money you choose is a stove, a box of matches and a couple gallons of gasoline. Now which stack seems more valuable?

If you're smart (and I know you are) you suddenly switch your choice of stacks again, right? Those Acme novelty bills are looking mighty attractive in terms of how they could be used, aren't they? The obvious point I'm getting at is that money only becomes valuable when it gets used, based on how it gets used. In addition to that, the less theoretical the situation is, the closer it is to a real-life need, the greater the value.

Now, in reality both stacks are imaginary, and you're not trapped in an arctic storm in the wilderness, somewhere outside Bethel, Alaska. The BIG idea here is why you should really want money. And it's also to demonstrate why money is not as valuable to you sitting in the bank. It might give you some peace of mind; some false notion that you're going to be protected when you stop working and that you're going to retire and live happily ever after (more on this in The "Golden Years" Trap).

But the reality is, this notion of "retirement as happily ever after" is the exception. Because, sure you have money sitting on a 401(k), IRA or retirement or savings account, But, when it's stored away like that, it won't produce more meaningful money — not in a way that will beat the pace of inflation. So, again, money is only valuable when it's used — based on how it gets used.

Like I hinted at in the beginning of this chapter, the banks spend their marketing dollars convincing you that you should keep the money you earn inside their control. The reason for that is simple: They want to do the exact thing with the money you give them that I'm telling you to do with it. They're *using* your money, not protecting it in a vault. And, naturally, they want your money for as cheap as they can get it. It pays them big dividends to get you to buy into their hustle of "safety net", "nest egg" and "happily ever after".

IT'S ALL SOMEONE ELSE'S

I want to be sure we're 100% clear about one thing. I'm not advising you to spend all your money. I'm too cheap myself to spend my earned money on things that don't produce more money. So, there's no way I'm encouraging you to "spend" money stupidly, not any more than I think you should be "saving" it stupidly, due to fear. Frivolous spending and feel-good purchases are even stupider, in most cases, than fear-based saving. So, let's use that to talk about the second rule...

THE 2ND RULE OF MONEY:

ALL MONEY IS REALLY SOMEONE ELSE'S

As I'm sitting here writing this, I'm looking at some sunglasses I own. It's a pair of high-end Versace shades that cost about $570. And sure, they protect my eyes and when I put them on, they probably make me look cool. But trading

$570 in earned income for something I could pay less than $5 for is just completely stupid to me.

I may scratch them. I might lose them. They'll almost definitely end up bent and sitting lopsided on my head, because that's what sunglasses do. So, I would never make that trade; $570 in earned income for a small chunk of plastic and metal. And this is a problem people run into because they take advice from new millionaires instead of wealthy multimillionaires or billionaires.

"NEVER TAKE ADVICE FROM MILLIONAIRES."

When a new millionaire gets their first little bit of money, they typically do one of two things. They either...

A. Spend it frivolously, thanks to stupidity or, more likely...
B. Enter scarcity mode and become over-protective of it due to fear, rather than using it to go out and get more money.

Ultimately people become complacent, especially in the middle-class comfort zone.

To test this out, ask ten people in the middle class, "Don't you want to make more money than you are right now?" I predict that what will happen is, 60% to 70% of them will respond with something along the lines of, "No I'm good.", even though the reality is probably that they can barely make ends meet. But if you press for verification, even though their response is not based on reality, they'll double down. You'll probably get something like, "I'm fine. Money's not everything." or "Money won't make me happy."

The real issue is, they've become complacent (whether they realize it or not) with what they "think" they have. But they're trying to protect something that's not even theirs, when what they should be doing is going out and getting more of it. And at the core of this flawed story, the biggest mistake they're making is believing that the money that they now have is theirs.

So, the question, as it relates to my $570 Versace shades is, "Was it worth it?" And the answer to that question depends on who you ask. Like I said, if I'd been foolish enough to trade $570 in earned income for that pair of sunglasses myself, I'd be in the "stupid" spending group. But the thing is, someone else bought them for me and gave them to me as a gift. He was a smart man, who understood the First and Second Rules of Money. So, he made the decision to give them to me as a gift, rather than keep the $570.

This is an example of the First Rule. Money is only valuable when it gets used — depending on how it gets used. If he had hoarded it out of fear, or if he had stupidly spent it on these shades for himself, he would be in breach of the first rule.

Instead, though, he chose to put the money to use, in line with the First Rule. He gave me the shades as a gift. He wrote them off as a tax deduction. He built his business because I know him now and he knows me. So, he invested in a high-level connection.

I now have an image of him as a good, generous, smart guy because he wisely spent $570 (of someone else's money) to give me a gift that I would likely never spend money on myself. And, again, that's important because of the Second Rule: All Money Is Really Someone Else's. It's never your money — every dollar that you may have today; all money that you have in the bank; all the money you'll have in the future — it's all someone else's money.

GO FORTH AND MULTIPLY

That gets us to the final of the three rules you need to know and follow if you're serious about going from left behind to rich to wealthy.

3RD RULE OF MONEY:

THE MONEY YOU EARN SHOULD ALWAYS MULTIFLY

To escape the middle-class money traps, you absolutely need income from different sources. And to make that point, I'll give you one example of how I approach anything and everything I do, when it comes to how I think about money.

When I host a conference, I always ask myself, "How do I create multiple flows of income with this?" For instance, I never assign one level of seat. I want a bunch of different seat levels, with revenue generated from multiple angles.

For instance, here's an "Ambassador" seat level at $95. Then there are "Hero" seats that I give away free to first responders, like fire fighters, police, military members and nurses. That's about $2.5M worth of seats I give away.

So, you might wonder, "But Grant, why would you give two and a half million dollars away if money's so valuable?" Fair question, but again, *money is only valuable when it's used, based on how it gets used.* This is an example of the principle behind Rule One.

To me, it's more valuable to show respect to the people who keep us all safe. I want 5,000, firefighters, nurses, policemen, members of the military, etc. in my audience. I'd rather make sure they're there and feel appreciated than directly make $2.5M by charging them for the seats.

See, to me, giving those seats away — while getting sponsors to pay for it, to help people that literally work their asses off every day and are underpaid constantly — is just good business. And naturally I have a real estate level, with its own section at $2,500, plus VIPs for $5,000 and Premier at $10K, with a Diamond level at $15K.

And then you might wonder why somebody would pay $15,000 for an event seat. Simple, they're smart enough to know the value of getting access to Kevin Hart, Tom Brady, Tillman Fertitta, Lloyd Blankfein, Usher, Alex Rodriguez, Floyd Mayweather, Snoop Dog, John Travolta, Megyn Kelly, Dana White and me. They are thinking, which all goes directly to the principle of "a lot of doors" from the first chapter. How do you create multiple entry points that give you multiple streams of income, with everything you do?

Starbucks has how many different types of beverages? They've got frappuccinos. They've got cappuccinos. They've got tea. They've got espressos, macchiatos, juices, five different types of water, plus merch!

What I've been trying to show in this section of the book is that you need to get multiple flows of income happening. Realize and remember that money has to be used; none of it is really yours and you've got to do everything you can to get it out of your savings and into investments that create multiple streams of income for you.

Start investing in assets that are real. View money as a weight around your neck if it's not going to make you more money. So, other than food, water and housing, all other money except for basic living, all other money should be put into things that are either tax deductible or tangible investments that will turn it into more money.

GO FOR BROKE

And as one final concept I want to pass on in this chapter, let's talk about the idea of becoming "broke". Most people focus all their attention on becoming rich. But the only way to become rich is to first become broke.

It's a pretty well-known fact about me that I go "broke" twice a year. The only reason to save money is to invest it. Put your saved money into secured, sacred (untouchable) accounts. Never use these accounts for anything, not even an emergency. To this day, I always invest my surpluses into ventures I cannot access. The reason for that is purely business, but it does go to the point about how to view cash versus "cash flow".

See, every business I create is specifically designed to do one thing — produce positive cash flow. If it doesn't perform that function, it does not exist in my world. And naturally that might mean I'm going to miss a bunch of potentially great "opportunities", like a Netflix type opportunity. I'm talking about the kinds of businesses that operate on negative cash flow for years, because they raise money (which is cash flow on somebody else's back, by the way).

For me though, that just doesn't work, because I know the truth. The vast majority of those types of opportunities fail. That's another topic that we'll get specific on in The "Over Diversification" Trap. But to me, people who invest in the stock market are gambling out of laziness. They haven't developed their work ethic.

The IRA, the 401(k), the retirement and pension funds, all of that on the other hand is just giving in to fear. When you go after those types of low yield investments, you're not investing yourself, possibly because you don't yet have the confidence in yourself. What you should do is invest in people and tangible assets that will produce you investment income.

I remember when I first told my mom that I was going to become a real estate investor. She asked me, "Why do you want to do that?" I told her, "Because I want to be rich. Remember I told you when I was 16 that I was going to be rich one day and help a lot of people?"

She said, "But Grant, you could have tenants calling you at midnight." And my response was, "I hope I do." "Why do you say that?" "Mom, what I don't want is people not calling me. I need that kind of contact and insight is I want to stay in touch with and in control of my business."

The bottom line here is, when you see hard work as the way forward rather than as an obstacle, you're so much better off than the kind of person who looks for the "easy" path or the "safe" route. A little bit of risk and a lot of hard work go a long way! And really, that's the point of this book. Because the truth behind the middle-class trap is that hard work alone can't get you from left behind to rich and then to wealthy. The banks and big companies want you to believe otherwise. They sell the idea of "Just work hard and everything will turn out alright." and "Save your money for a rainy day."

"IF YOU DON'T FIND A WAY TO MAKE MONEY WHILE YOU SLEEP, YOU WILL WORK UNTIL YOU DIE."

- WARREN BUFFETT

But the truth is really that there's a huge difference between "earned" income and "investment" income. Your job, wherever you work, whether your salary is $60K or $600K a year, that's earned income. It's the highest taxed income there is. And unfortunately, it's very difficult to create wealth, not impossible, but very difficult to create true financial freedom and real wealth with earned income alone.

Investment income though, like a multi-unit apartment complex you can pour literally all your free money into. Real assets, hard assets like physical properties that create cash flow, that type of investment income is the lowest taxed, with the best tax advantages and the best chances of providing you with appreciation over long periods of time.

That's investment income. It's how you get from left behind to rich, then from rich to wealthy. That's why I pour all my money back into hard assets like those that really can't easily lose the money, while still producing positive cash flow.

In Section Four: The Wealth Creation Formula, I'm going to give you the specific details on how to create wealth by finding the right vehicle (not a car, a financial vehicle). I'll also show you how the "Circle of Three" works.

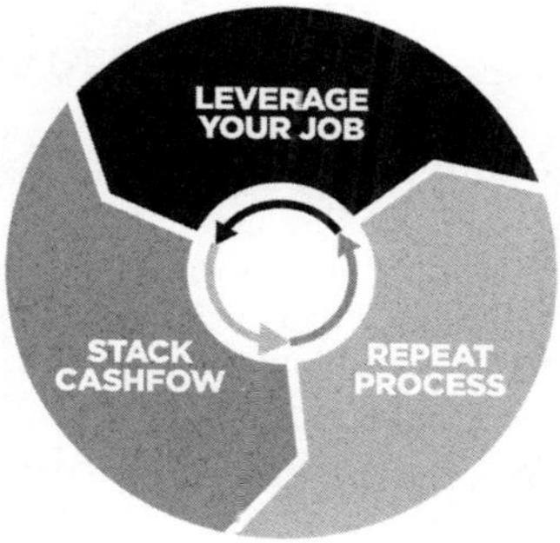

The Circle of Three:

First: Leverage your job situation as a base

Second: Stack an additional cash-flow opportunity on top of that to increase your income.

Third: Repeat that process until things stabilize enough to make your next bracket jump

THE "PIGGY BANK" ASSESSMENT QUESTIONS:

1. **How much do you currently have saved?**
   - A. None (4)
   - B. Less than $10,000 (3)
   - C. Between $10,000 and $100,000 (2)
   - D. More than $100,000 (1)

2. **How much interest is the money you're saving currently earning?**
   - A. 0% (4)
   - B. Some, but less than 5% (3)
   - C. Between 5% and 10% (2)
   - D. More than 10% (1)

3. **How much are you currently generating in passive income?**
   - A. None (5)
   - B. Less than $1,000 (4)
   - C. Between $1,000 and $5,000 (3)
   - D. Between $5,000 and $10,000 (2)
   - E. More than $10,000 (1)

4. **How many passive income streams do you have**
   - A. 0 (4)
   - B. 1-3 (3)
   - C. 3-10 (2)
   - D. More than 10 (1)

TOTAL SCORE:

** These scores will be addressed in Section Four: The Wealth Creation Formula.*

III. The "Plastic" Trap

By the end of this chapter, my goal is to get you to understand the real problem with using credit cards the wrong way: I know it can help you, not only to become more financially fit, but also to improve your physical fitness. I'll show you:

1. **Why you should go on a 6-month credit card "fast"** (This is more than a novelty or a strongly worded challenge)

2. **How going without credit cards can make you less fat** (seriously, it can drastically improve your physical fitness)

3. **When it's the right time to start using credit cards again**

JUST A THOUSAND HOURS

As human beings, we take so many things for granted. I lost my dad when I was 10. I lost my older brother when I was 20. I talked to him on a Monday night and boom he was gone on Tuesday before I woke up.

When I was 10 and they took my dad off to Houston from our home in Louisiana, I thought he was coming back. He never did. He was in intensive care for 21 days. The day they were going to release him he died. He only made two requests of my mother on his deathbed: "Take care of those boys and tell them to learn how to sell."

I spent maybe a thousand hours total with my dad my entire life. But in those thousand hours, he taught me so much. And there were three big things that have really stayed with me.

CURTIS CARDONE LESSON #1 - WORK HARD: First, he ingrained in me hard work. He never sat me down and said, "Hey Grant, let's have a talk about hard work." It was through his actions. My Dad's eyes could be bleeding and he'd still show up for work, zero excuses. He believed it was his duty; his obligation to his wife, to his five kids, to his parents and his brothers and extended family.

CURTIS CARDONE LESSON #2 - PROTECT YOUR REPUTATION: The second thing he taught me was about protecting my reputation, especially by way of acknowledging people. He talked to everyone. He never said, "Hey Grant, make sure you talk to everybody. Pay attention to everybody." He just set that example. He told me that my name was everything. Protect your name. The most valuable thing you have is your name and the reputation associated with it.

CURTIS CARDONE LESSON #3 - DON'T RELY ON CREDIT: The third and maybe most important thing he taught me was to live within my means and pay in full for everything. He never bought anything on credit; not a car; not a house; nothing. The rule was, save up and when you can do it, pay the full price.

Toward the end of his life, I think he knew he was going to be leaving, so he was trying to sock away as much money as he could. And I know that a lot of people out there have parents who planned on retiring by now. Instead, though, they find themselves unable to do that. Maybe they're still underwater with their home, unable to sell it. Or maybe they've lost their job.

Someone I know just told me about her friend's parents, who are 63 and 65 years old. Her 63-year-old mother lost her job a year and a half ago and they've been trying to make ends meet for a year and a half. Then, this past week her 65-year-old father lost his job. Naturally, they weren't planning on that.

People who have fallen into the middle-class trap believe that they will be in the same job for years. They think they are secure and they will be alright. They also hope for things like 6% to 8% interest rates on their savings accounts, which they just won't get.

The variables that helped create the middle class do not exist anymore. So many people, like my friend's parents, end up living on their credit cards because there's no other way to keep up. But credit cards are so dangerous in that scenario.

FOOLISH, FAT AND FORGETFUL

It's not just a strongly worded alliteration to say, "credit cards make you foolish, fat and forgetful." There are documented studies that prove all three are true. But, even more than that, credit cards can make you a slave. There's a concerted effort for us to become a "plastic" society and it's happening because people cannot discipline themselves.

Most human beings don't yet have a mechanism for handling the impulse that naturally gets triggered when using cards. Visa, MasterCard and American Express understand and leverage this impulse. So do the department stores. Why else do you think that when you're trying to buy something at one of those places for the first time, they beg you to take their credit card? They offer to pay you to take their credit cards because they know if you have plastic, you'll purchase things you didn't want and you don't need — things you know are bad for you.

The bank's want us weak. The retailers want you packing those cards, because they know you can be tempted by that plastic.

That's exactly the reason we're becoming a cashless society — a world where physical money is nearly obsolete. In the 1970s, fewer than 20% of the entire adult population had a credit card. Today that number is over 80%. Don't believe me? Try to purchase an airline ticket today and they'll tell you, "We only accept credit cards."

Sweden has a national effort underway to take their country cashless. And that's why I want to challenge you to operate without credit cards for 6 months — not for the rest of your life — just for the next six months. Let me help you build credit card spending muscles. For six months though, leave the plastic out of the equation.

"Credit cards will turn you into a fool!"

FOOLISH: Credit cards are actually causing irresponsibility. They're actually linked to people being irresponsible. The typical knock-on credit cards is that they're too easy to use. They let you buy stuff you don't need. If you had to reach in your pocket and pay with physical money, you might not make the same decision. But with a credit card, you whip out little plastic, slide it, spank it across your fingers hoping it goes through and you can wait 30 days and pay.

MIT conducted a study where they organized an auction for the Boston Celtics. They gave one group of people cash. They gave another group of people credit cards. Guess who bid up the tickets the most? Right, the people with credit cards. And not only did they bid the auction up the most, but they also paid double what people without credit cards paid.

And when it comes to the idea of building credit with credit cards, the reality is painfully obvious. There are over 1 billion

Visa, Mastercard, and Amex cards in circulation just in the United States. Many people let credit card companies use them, rather than using the credit card companies as a convenient accounting device. It is unnecessary for anyone to ever find themselves the victim of their credit cards, but people are paying late fees, penalties, and high-interest rates, because they have no discipline. Today, credit card interest rates are as high as 24%. That's insane. Allowing credit card debt to snowball at those interest rates is a formula to *destroy* wealth in your life.

The problem is most Americans don't make enough income so they can't pay off their expenditures. Spending $4 on a cup of coffee is fine, unless you only earn $12 an hour — but that's not a credit problem, it's an income problem. You do want some debt in your life, because not all debt is bad — but nobody needs credit frivolous card debt.

"Visa, Amex and Mastercard make you fat"

FAT: Research also shows that people with credit cards are actually more frequently obese than people who don't have credit cards. MIT also conducted a research study and found that people that use credit cards ended up with unhealthy products that expand their waistband instead of their wallet. The shopping baskets of people that were paying cash actually had higher nutritional items and lower fat items.

The disorder you see in a person's external physical life can tell you so much about their financial situation. I find it very interesting how many people who seem to be out of control with their physical health live on credit today. As an example, just the other day I went to the theater to catch a movie. I hit the first show of the opening weekend Sunday, because I know there won't be a big crowd. When I get to the theater, there's a woman in front of me who seems to be having troubles in life. She's an extremely obese woman, there with her boyfriend, who you can just tell doesn't really love or respect her the way a man should.

To paint the picture for you, this woman isn't dressed well. Her clothes aren't in good condition. Her purse isn't in good condition. And she goes to the movie with her boyfriend who lets her pay for both of their tickets – with her credit card. Then they make a beeline straight to the concession stand and load up with what had to be $50 worth of goodies.

Other than acknowledging the pain she must have in her life, I didn't give it much thought past making the observation. I went straight to my seat without stopping at the concession stand. Then this couple sits down right next to me. They're bickering about her buying the wrong snacks, of all things.

Her boyfriend, who's also overweight, is making her feel bad about the choices of snacks she purchased with her credit card – snacks neither of them needs. Her defense against this complaining is that she was trying to save money. So, she then goes into her purse and pulls out a bunch of stuff she snuck in from her house trying to be thrifty.

I'm just amazed at this credit card epidemic and how many people are living on credit cards. Whether your spouse is the credit card junkie or you're the credit card junkie I want you to get rid of your credit cards.

There are really 4 Flags of the Plastic Trap:

1. **You can't make it a month without relying on plastic:** If you're relying on credit cards to buy necessities or, God forbid, things like movie tickets and snacks – STOP.

2. **You can barely make your monthly payment:** You'll end up paying a ton in interest and it will take a whole lot longer to pay your cards off (NOTE: this doesn't mean paying extra toward your cards and still using them)

3. **You're using cards to purchase stuff you can't otherwise afford:** If you don't need it and you can't afford it but you're thinking about paying for it with plastic — DON'T!

4. **You're reaching your card limits:** This sin means you're probably relying on credit cards to live and that is NOT living at all!

If you are waving any of these four flags, it means it's time for a credit card fast. no matter how painful it might seem. Believe me when I say going on a credit card fast will be far less painful than the inevitable fate you will suffer if you don't. Because credit cards create an illusion of liquidity that you don't actually possess. They make you forget the reality of your financial situation.

FORGETFUL: It's like you got hit on the head and have "money amnesia". I know people who actually think credit cards are their income. They buy things at the store, then later say it didn't cost them anything because they put it on their card. They forget the connection between their actual money and these little plastic cards, as if they're some sort of magic wand.

"CREDIT CARDS GIVE YOU AMNESIA ABOUT YOUR REAL MONEY SITUATION"

Why do you think Bloomingdale's, Saks Fifth Avenue and Macy's want to give you their plastic? Because they want you to be slaves. They want to disconnect you from your financial reality, so you forget and overspend. Like a drug dealer who gives you drugs for free, so you get that first little taste. He wants to turn you into a junkie.

I've had a Visa card for 30 years, but I have never paid one penny in interest — not one penny. The reason for that is simple: I pay my cards off every month. The fact is credit card companies don't actually make most of their money from interest. It's from the late fees. That's why they want you to be late. Their goal is to make you feel like a terrible human being so they can justify making money the way they really do it.

They want you to be late, because when you are, you're really their best customer. They're really thinking, "Could you please continue to be late more often, but not too late, just late enough to pay us? We love it! You just gave us the perfect justification to jack your rate up!"

You don't think the drug dealer's going to tell you they want you addicted to their junk, do you? The first time they share a little snort with you, they're going to act nice and harmless. Once you're reliant on their supply though, it's a whole different story. Drug dealers love you to stress out. That way you need more of their supply. Banks and credit card companies are exactly the same. Unfortunately, I know all the patterns because of my history with substance abuse.

So, when I ask you to give up using credit cards for six months, I'm not suggesting that you should never use them again. What I'm saying is, until you develop the extreme discipline required to properly handle using credit cards, you should resist them. Treat them just like you would any narcotic: Visa, MasterCard, American Express and Discovery included!

This is one of the lessons of the middle class, particularly my father's generation, that's still in use today. Many of the things that previous generations did in their era, cannot work today, because the variables have changed. But one thing they did extremely well was not use plastic the way we do today. And that's what I'm looking for from anyone I work with. I want the people I work with solving their own problems, because if you come to work with me and you expect me to solve your problem, you're not an asset, you're actually a liability.

I have zero debt, because I want true freedom — to be able to move and come and go as I please. You want freedom too, right? You don't want to be stuck or frozen, so don't let yourself be the concrete sidewalk that other people walk on. You're a human being and you deserve to be free.

Still, while you don't need to use a credit card to improve your credit rating, you should definitely have at least one or two credit cards to operate in modern society. And if your job or business requires travel, that's completely different than paying for movie tickets, popcorn, soda and 32 ounces of Raisinets, like the lady and her boyfriend in line ahead of me at the theater. They did not need to use credit for stuff like that. Way too many people don't have their heads wrapped around how to use credit. They have their credit muscles trained totally wrong.

As an example, I recently had a guy who owes me money, and rather than paying me, he went and picked up the new iPhone. He doesn't owe me a lot of money, but he owes me more than twice the amount of that iPhone. I have another person who owes me $700K and he's out buying expensive cars and boats instead of paying me. That's two different people who have forgotten how important their credit and the reputation related to it are.

And really the reason I'm pressing you to get rid of your credit cards for the next six months is so you can get your priorities in order. First thing to do when you've got debts is pay them off, before creating any new debt. Because you don't want your attention on owing people money. Then, once your attention is off of that, you can go get some new money.

The real problem is so many people will pay back the bank or they'll pay college loans or they'll pay back the government, of course, but they won't pay back their friends. How ridiculous is that? People will pay back the people they don't like before they pay back the people that they work with, partner with and love — or at least the people they say they love.

Paying off debts has to start somewhere and to me the best place to start isn't as much with "who" you pay back, it's to stop building debt with the people you supposedly care the least about. Stop creating debt with the department stores, the banks and the credit card companies, right now — TODAY!

There isn't one human being on this planet who I owe a penny to. That's the reason I'm able to go out and create new income. If you want to be free of the middle-class traps, and start creating wealth for yourself, one of the most important steps you've got to take is cleaning up your past liabilities. Go clean it up. And the only way to clean it up is to pay it off and pay it back. Don't sweep it underneath the carpet. Make the decision right now to go on a 6-month credit card fast.

And right now, make sure you answer these five questions, so your Wealth Creation Formula gets fully developed.

THE "PLASTIC" TRAP
ASSESSMENT QUESTIONS:

1. **How often do you use "plastic" to buy non-essentials or luxuries?**
   - A. Never (1)
   - B. Sometimes (2)
   - C. All the time (3)

2. **How much non-disciplined credit card debt do you currently have?**
   - A. None (1)
   - B. Less than $1,000 (2)
   - C. Between $1,000 and $10,000 (3)
   - D. Between $10,000 and $50,000 (4)
   - E. More than $50,000 (5)

3. **How many credit cards do you currently have that are near or at the balance limit?**
   - A. 0 (1)
   - B. 1-2 (2)
   - C. 3-10 (3)
   - D. More than 10 (4)

4. **How confident are you about doing a 6-month credit card fast?**
   - A. Not confident at all (3)
   - B. Slightly confident (2)
   - C. Very confident (1)

5. **Which of the 4 Flags of the Plastic Trap are true for you?**
   - ☐ You can't make it a month without relying on plastic (1)
   - ☐ You can barely make your monthly payments (1)
   - ☐ You're using cards to for stuff you can't otherwise afford (1)
   - ☐ You're reaching your card limits (1)

TOTAL SCORE:

** These scores will be addressed in Section Four: The Wealth Creation Formula.*

Section Two: "EDUCATION" TRAPS

Section Summary: In this second section you'll get clear on the three common pitfalls related to "education".

IV. The "Higher Education" Trap
Where you're told to believe in the idea that you need a paper degree from an institution of "higher learning" if you want to be successful

V. The "Millionaire Next Door" Trap
The trap of believing that there is a set of common traits that show up again and again among those who have accumulated wealth. And that most of the truly wealthy in this country don't live in Beverly Hills or on Park Avenue — they live next door

VI. The "Misinformation" Trap
In which the beliefs you've developed and accumulated from your family, friends, the media and institutional education prevent you from achieving true wealth

A couple of these traps may not be what you'd probably expect when I use the phrase "education trap". Believe me when I tell you that they are all directly related to education. And these are all traps that you want to either avoid or escape from as quickly as possible.

IV.
The "Higher Education" Trap

This fourth middle-class trap often leads to several of the other traps. And it keeps you from creating wealth. In this chapter, you'll find out...

1. **Why the math doesn't work** (when it comes to building real wealth, what you pay for a university degree, just doesn't ROI)

2. **Which skills you really need to learn** (depending on your role as an employee, freelancer or business owner)

3. **The single most important class missing from EVERY university curriculum**

After reading this chapter, you get clear on what you really need to focus on when it comes to a "higher education" and it's NOT the things you probably think it is, based on the misinformation you've probably had access to so far.

THE "PAPER" JUST DON'T PENCIL OUT

I went to college and got a five-year degree. It wasn't worth anything to me. I'm not saying it's not worth something, I'm saying it wasn't worth anything to me. I didn't have the right ideas about it. I went to get an accounting degree. I thought that an accounting degree was going to make me money. School didn't teach me anything about making money though. I got out of college and, like a lot of people, I couldn't even get a job. I remember having no money, only debt and no belief in myself.

So, when it comes to the "Higher Education" trap, the question is simple: "Is that paper degree a path to creating wealth? Or is it a trap?" Don't get me wrong. I'm not knocking a formal education across the board. The problem is it lacks the practical side, the fundamentals of financial literacy; how to build strong relationships; how to increase your income or build a business. So, if it doesn't teach you any of that core stuff that's key to making, keeping and multiplying your money, is it really worth spending hundreds of thousands of dollars to attend classes at an institution that won't give you the basic knowledge you need to create wealth?

Too many people get stuck on this idea that to be successful you have to go to school, get a degree, get a good job, and you know the rest. But it's been proven that, not only do you not have to attend school to be successful, but you can also learn everything you need to know online. You can start an entire successful online business selling products and services. You can teach yourself new skills that people will pay the big bucks for. You can replace a full-time income and triple the amount you make by selling your skills online. So why would you need a traditional or formal college education?

Some of the most expensive universities can cost around $75,000 per year. I went to college, got a five-year degree, and it's ridiculous because it isn't worth anything to me. Now, I say again, I don't want you to think that I'm saying school isn't worth it in general. It certainly can be for those who want specific training in careers related to finance, medicine, law and the like.

What I am saying is that, for a lot of people, it doesn't provide them with the skills required to actually make money or build a life of wealth. Most of the time, education can accumulate more debt than your credit card and gives you a piece of paper that doesn't have as much meaning as it used to. For me, I didn't go in with the right mindset or the right intentions. I went and got an accounting degree. I thought it was going to give me something useful about business but low and behold, it didn't teach me anything about business.

So, is that paper degree really worth it? Once I graduated, I had a tough time trying to land a job. Like most new graduates, they leave with a fancy degree, but have the most difficult time finding work because it's competitive out there and they don't have any real experience. It's an epidemic. People are hungry for knowledge. They want information. The problem here is that this information is all about "How do I get a job?" and not "How do I become an entrepreneur?"

This, more than anything else, really defines the middle-class trap. The reality is, we're taught to make our money, save it, and conserve it as much as possible. By this mindset, sooner or later, you will run out of money. This isn't freedom. What we need to understand is that no matter where you're at in life, you need to learn how to make more money, how to increase your income, how to create multiple streams of income, how to sell, how to network and so on.

A "VERY PARTICULAR SET OF SKILLS"

I don't care who you are, there is something you do better than anyone else. Whether you're aware of it, you've got some solid money-making skills in the works. And not to get all Liam Neeson on you, but we all have a "particular set of skills."

More than likely, you already have a skill in mind you are looking to monetize. The problem is that not everyone knows how to use their strengths to make money.

For example, you know the number one reason why businesses fail? They can't sell enough — not well enough, not fast enough, and not in large enough quantities to sustain themselves. As a result, you see starving artists, broke solopreneurs and small businesses closing their doors. Let's turn the tide in the other direction — starting with YOU. So, here's a simplified, yet specific breakdown of how developing money-making skills could apply to you, depending on what role or roles you're in:

EMPLOYEE: I can tell you that I am always on the lookout for talent. A competent employee is worth their weight in gold to me — and any other smart business owner, for that matter. As an employee, selling your abilities to your superiors is your ultimate bargaining chip. It allows you to negotiate raises and promotions, gives you the freedom to choose your own projects and makes you indispensable.

My best people have grown with my companies because they have played to their strengths using skills that make money. A shining example of this is the President of Cardone Enterprises, Jarrod Glandt. He started out as a sales guy for me and climbed his way to being my right-hand man.

FREELANCER: Freelancers are mini-business owners in and of themselves. Consequently, the above reasons apply to them as well. Additionally, freelancers need to maximize their skills to make money because often their "company" is just them. Honing in on how lucrative your ability is can be the difference between struggling and affluence.

For example, the difference in pay between a general transcriptionist and a court stenographer is huge. The general transcriptionist earns about $43,000 a year, while the latter has an average salary of around $57,000. That's an extra $14,000 a year! An understanding of how valuable your skill set is positions you as a professional — and everyone is looking for an expert.

BUSINESS OWNER: Business owners should absolutely be leveraging the money-making skills they have. Think about the longest-standing and most profitable companies of all time. Microsoft. Ford. Apple. All their founders were the best at what they did, then translated those skills into something marketable.

Creating a business from something you are knowledgeable about maintains its sustainability. A strong business starts from the top. So, this also establishes your authority as a leader when you are proficient in your field. In other words, it's easier to keep a business running if you know what you're doing.

Regardless of which category you fall into, you are going to implement some — if not all — of the strategies below to monetize your skills.

SOME VALUABLE SKILLS TO DEVELOP

Now that you know the why, here is the how. And, as you read, you may notice something all these tactics have in common. These ideas are ALL forms of promotion. Money follows attention, so get creative with the strategies below to get more money for your skills:

PERSONAL BRANDING: In this age of information, building a powerful personal brand is more than a buzzword. It's the foundation for effectively monetizing your talents. Social media gives everyone the chance to promote themselves in their area of expertise.

It is plain stupid to not use this tool to your full advantage. Blogs, YouTube videos, and podcasts are all effective — and FREE — ways to develop a personal brand. This allows people to see what you can do, as opposed to you telling them. And I hate to break it to you, but no one is going to take you at your word that your skill set is worth paying for... People want to do business with people they like and know. Strong branding makes that connection easier.

AFFILIATE MARKETING: One of the benefits of establishing yourself as an authority is the ability to take part in affiliate marketing. In this type of partnership, you receive money to feature or demonstrate a product to your online audience. This practice has existed as long as marketing has been around. However, social media has made this opportunity more accessible.

Some "influencers" generate massive income from this strategy alone. But there are specific rules around this type of marketing. Research all the regulations and brands you plan on partnering with before you take the plunge. That being said, affiliate marketing is still a legit way to put your money-making skills into action.

COURSE CREATION: The ultimate testament to one's skills is being able to teach them to another. So, why not get paid for it? Publishing an online course allows you to do just that. Plus, it means you can reach a larger audience than you could teaching one on one. There are a ton of platforms and ways to get your course online. But the most important part is structuring and creating the content so people can learn it effectively. That part is up to you. People want knowledge, and they want it from the best. If you can write a course that others can use to become successful, everyone wins.

COACHING/CONSULTING: When you're known as THE "guy" or "gal" in your field, people will want to monopolize your time so you can focus on solving their problems. This is a big opportunity for you to apply your money-making skills as a coach or consultant. It's no secret that people pay big money for celebrity personal trainers, interior designers, or even doctors.

You can use this method to make money in your area of expertise as well. And don't worry. You don't need to establish yourself as a Dr. Oz to be successful as a consultant. You've just got to know the specific individuals you can help and offer your services to them. Word about your ability to help will ultimately translate into increased rates for your time and advice.

PLATFORM SPEAKING: If you needed a sign to get over stage fright, here it is. Public speaking is a strong method for you to make money with what you do best. I know because I did it, for years. This route to monetize your skills is no get-rich-quick scheme. It takes development. You have to build a reputation so people know you are worth coming out to see.

Before establishing myself, I did too many free speaking engagements to count. I didn't do it for the money at first. I did it to get out and prove myself. And because I put in the work and my content was effective, I now have workshops priced at thousands of dollars a ticket. You can do the same. You just have to be willing to step out of your comfort zone and onto the stage. Regardless of your specialty, public speaking is an underrated and profitable way to promote yourself.

VIRTUAL EVENT HOSTING: In the same way getting on public stages can help you earn an income, you can do the same by hosting your own events. In-person and virtual events are equally powerful in bolstering your message. Any kind of event helps you foster a community of people interested in your brand. Today, most social networking sites have options to go "live," which you can use to your advantage.

Those who are already interested in you can check out what you have to say and easily refer others. You can earn revenue by charging for these events or segue into selling another one of your products. Either way, gathering like-minded people will create opportunities to make money.

BOOK AUTHORING: First of all, book writing has been a big part of my career, and it continues to be to this day. I've published multiple bestsellers in the process which have helped countless people around the world. I wrote *Sell or Be Sold* to teach other salespeople the step-by-step process that no one ever showed me when I started out. Then, I wrote *How to Create Wealth Investing in Real Estate* to share the investing strategies which worked for me.

Whenever I write a book, it is to show my steps for success. In turn, those books have become bestsellers. Therefore, if you have a great collection of life lessons and resources to offer, get them out on paper. Not only is it an effective way to push your money-making skills, but you'll also provide a unique experience for your readers.

E-COM MARKETING: As far as I can tell, everyone loves merch. For that reason, you might want to consider opening an e-commerce store. With a little creativity, you can design merchandise tailored to your brand. From hot sauce to aviation, people like showing off their interests through clothing, bumper stickers and so on.

An e-commerce store provides an official source from which your audience can get these items. Also, if you took my advice from the section above, it gives you a place to sell your book without having to give a cut to another retailer. Generating revenue through e-commerce will just continue to grow as time goes on. Don't miss the opportunity to use it to your advantage.

SELLING: Last and definitely not least, the unrivaled technique to start cashing in on your skills is to learn to sell. You have to be able to convince others you are as good as you know you are. Let's look back at the three roles we talked about earlier: the business owner, freelancer and employee. An integral part of any of them monetizing their skills is their ability to sell others on their value.

"MASTER SALES, AND THE WORLD WILL BE YOUR OYSTER!"

Business owners have to sell customers on their products or services, otherwise the business will fail. Freelancers have to sell their potential clients on the superiority of their skills, otherwise, the clients will choose another contractor. And unless employees can sell their value to the company, they will find themselves overlooked for promotions — or even worse, out of a job. Sales is not just for "salespeople." It is a critical skill you need to be successful in any area of life. Master sales, and the world will be your oyster!

I know all this may seem a little bit overwhelming. Make sure you're clear that these are all just options. These are some tools that are important to successfully monetize your skills. So, as an example of how to use these as combos, let me use my own application...

Let's start with a personal brand. When social media first came out, I was criticized for flooding the various platforms with posts and content. Nonetheless, I knew I had to get my name out there. The result is now I have a strong brand approaching 17 million+ followers across my social media platforms.

Don't you think that's allowed me to reach more people? Yep!

Early on, I also wrote a course based on my sales technology (Cardone U). You know what that's allowed me to do? I've been able to help tens of thousands of people and hundreds of companies increase their revenue. That's something I'm super proud of. And before that, I was going around the country doing public speaking engagements and events teaching my content. These workshops and speaking gigs were my entire business model for many years. Honestly, it was very profitable, but I could only reach and help a limited number of people using that model.

And you know, throughout my entire career, I've written books. The books themselves sold extremely well. More importantly, though, they got attention. But sales was where it all started. Once I committed to getting good at sales — which I hated at first — everything changed. I wasn't struggling to pay the $275 rent on my crappy apartment anymore. I could feed my dog and myself.

At the time, that was as much success as I could imagine. Becoming proficient in sales continues to fuel my success to this day. At the end of the day, no matter where you are in your career, learning to make money from your abilities is the way to long-term, sustainable success.

THE BOTTOM LINE

Here's the slightly harsh truth: If you're not reaching your full potential every day, you are "broke" right now. I want you to think really hard about whether a formal education is the right solution. It can be right for you depending on what it is you want as a career. But, if you're any of the following:

- A visionary...
- A big thinker...
- Someone who loves to create...
- Someone who wants more out of life...
- Someone who wants passive income...
- Someone who wants to multiply their income...
- Someone who wants to build a life that only very few people are willing to sacrifice to make happen...

Then I know for a fact, school will hold you back. And, if you don't want to stress about your finances, your job, whether you'll have a job the next day, or if you can keep your current home, you absolutely don't want to put yourself in a position where you can't enjoy your life. So, let's jump back to that original question that I started this chapter with...

Is that paper degree really worth it? The reality is, you can be a better person when you're not constantly bogged down by your financial situation. You can achieve so much more when you're not getting frustrated with your partner over money or feeling like a victim to your circumstances. So, is that paper degree really worth it? Not if you want to live a life of freedom. It's your choice. Decide what life you want and travel down that path. Only you can decide what is best for you.

I wish I would have gone to Harvard, but NOT for the degree. I wish I would have gone for the connections. I also wish I would have paid more attention when I was going to college. Unfortunately for me — and so many others — I had no direction as it relates to why I was there. I had no specific purpose for what I was learning, so I left my university with a piece of paper, debt, no idea about my future and very few skills.

You don't need college to get rich. And the problem isn't in education. It's in the approach. When you approach an education, you have to think about skills, not just information or knowledge. Only 27 percent of college graduates are even working in the field they studied. One of the reasons you should study is to gain skills. The only things you can use every day to bring more value to the marketplace are your skills. And everyone must learn sales, but no major university teaches it.

I remember seeing my old high school recently and to this day, it looks like a prison from the outside. I was forced to go to classes I didn't want to be in. Things like History, Geography, Algebra and English grammar (whatever that was about) and I was forced to read books I had zero interest in. Shop class was OK. Typing class was good because Ms. Gardner was hot. But overall, public school was NOT a great learning experience for me.

And, while I wasn't the Homecoming King, I was runner-up in my senior class for "Mr. Vogue". Unfortunately, 1st place went to a guy named Buc Gregory. You read that right. I lost the Mr. Vogue title to a guy named Buc! But you know what? The good thing about high school is, it doesn't determine how your life turns out. While I may have been fashionable to get 2nd place as Mr. Vogue, I had no clue how to make any money. That's because nobody in high school taught me how to increase my income. And neither did anyone in college!

I didn't get wealthy from what I learned in school. I became wealthy because of what I chose to learn after school. Never stop learning and educating yourself. I read every day, study, skill up and work to stay ahead of the competition and the trends in the market. I didn't go to Princeton, Brown, Yale, Stanford, MIT, Cambridge or Harvard. I actually went to a small school called McNeese State University, surrounded by oak trees in Lake Charles, Louisiana. I just needed a GPA of 2.35 for admission – which is equivalent to around a C. Just don't completely fail and drop out of high school and you can get into McNeese State. University for me — and many others — is basically a path to the middle class, not to teach you a formula for creating wealth. You don't go to school to become a millionaire or billionaire. If the goal of higher education is to be financially secure, then it is failing miserably.

REMEMBER THOSE SKILLS

When you approach schooling, you've got to think about gaining skills necessary for creating wealth, not just collecting information or knowledge. We need more skilled people, not more educated people. We need motivated workers — and motivation comes from having skills. Great entrepreneurs, salespeople and successful people that get results aren't born great. They're educated (the right way), motivated and trained to be where they're at. There are millionaires being made every day, but you aren't going to learn the information you need to become one from any school system — not even Harvard.

How do I know this? Because Harvard doesn't even have classes on increasing your income. The ROI on good, real-world business training is much higher than any MBA program in the country. With growing tuition debt and the lack of any real-world benefit from spending four years at college, more and more people are turning to online education. It's easier to be one-click away from information and people don't want to be fed a business or marketing curriculum that was put together in 1997.

There are millionaires being made each day in this country, and you don't need to go to college to become one of them. If you want a superior education at an affordable price that prepares you for the real world, get on Cardone University, my platform for teaching people the real skills they need to succeed in business, sales and life. The ROI will be much higher, and you don't need to go into student loan debt.

THE "HIGHER EDUCATION" TRAP ASSESSMENT QUESTIONS:

1. **Have you attended a college or university?**
   A. Yes (2)
   B. No (1)

If you answered "No" to the above, enter total score of "1" below.

2. **How many years of paid higher education did you attend?**
   A. Less than one year (1)
   B. Less than two years (2)
   C. I got my 2-year degree (3)
   D. I got my 4-year degree (4)
   E. I got a 6-year degree or higher (5)

3. **How much did your college education cost you in total?**
   A. Less than $50K (1)
   B. More than $50K (2)
   C. Over $100K (3)
   D. Over $200K (4)

4. **Do you feel like your degree was worth the work and financial cost?**
   A. Yes (2)
   B. No (1)

5. **What skills do you feel like you missed that you'd like to develop?**
   - ☐ Sales (1)
   - ☐ Marketing (1)
   - ☐ Team Building (1)
   - ☐ Leadership (1)

TOTAL SCORE:

** These scores will be addressed in Section Four: The Wealth Creation Formula.*

V.
The "Millionaire Next Door" Trap

This fifth trap would have you believing that there is a set of common traits that show up again and again among those who have accumulated wealth. And that most of the truly wealthy in this country don't live in Beverly Hills or on Park Avenue — they live next door. This chapter will help you see things like...

1. **Why listening to a millionaire kills wealth creation**

2. **How to think about money so you never need to worry**

3. **The real reason you want BIGGER problems!**

Read this chapter only if you're ready to believe that making a million dollars can actually be an impedance to becoming truly wealthy.

DON'T LISTEN TO MILLIONAIRES

It was early spring, 1997. The voice of Captain James T. Kirk was beginning to blow up the airwaves. Suddenly, you couldn't make the morning rush-hour drive to work without hearing the voice of actor William Shatner on the radio. The topic? A new travel booking website about to launch, called Priceline.com.

The agency that was handling the radio air spot purchases had to deliver some bad news to Jay Walker, Priceline's founder. "Your tech team says that the ads are too popular. The website is set to go live in three days and they say it won't be able to handle the traffic that the radio spots are generating. They tell me we should hold off on the launch until we can beef up the tech. What do you want to do Jay?"

After thinking about it briefly, reflecting on the potential embarrassment of the website crashing for millions of people, Walker made the decision anyone who understands "wealth creation" would make. "Double the ads", he calmly replied. The rest, as they say, is history. Priceline went on to make billions, creating an entire industry for discounted travel and lodging booking.

And I don't tell you this story because I love Priceline or William Shatner so much. It's because there's a way that someone who's truly thinking right about money behaves and responds. There's a degree of "unworry" that they manage to achieve. That's the difference in the way a billionaire thinks, versus a millionaire.

All that said, there was a best-selling book written years ago called *The Millionaire Next Door*. I can tell you the only thing I learned from the book was that I didn't want to be The Millionaire Next Door. *The Millionaire Next Door* basically suggests that if you are frugal, you can be a millionaire someday. And that most of the wealthy don't live in Beverly Hills or Park Avenue, but next to you, under the radar.

It goes on to preach that there are seven common traits among millionaires that you can copy to get there, too. Now, this book has sold millions and millions of copies. It was a bestseller. One of the reasons I believe it was is that it has little tiny specks of truth as bait set on a giant misinformation trap (more on this in The "Misinformation" Trap). But the simple truth is, despite the book being read by millions, most Americans still do NOT have an under-the-radar millionaire next door to them. And they're not on any path to become a millionaire themselves.

Why is that? Because the book miseducates people who are looking for the path to become wealthy. The truth is, *The Millionaire Next Door* will leave you old and angry. That's because it fundamentally miseducates you about what wealth really is.

Everyone uses the word "wealth". Most people say they want wealth. But do you actually know what "wealth" means? If you want wealth in your life, you have to know what it is. Wealth is having more than enough of everything that is vital to your survival. Wealth is not dependent on one thing — the limit of a bank account, a car, a house, a job, a relationship — it's having *more* than enough of everything that you want and need. It's abundance and affluence.

Notice that wealth does *not* include worry. Yet, a lot of you are worried right now. 76% of all Americans are living paycheck to paycheck in the richest country in the world. Maybe you're worried about whether you can afford five-dollar coffee, picking up the check at a restaurant or about student loans, or maybe you're worried about paying that 30-year mortgage or about paying your kid's school tuition.

Chances are you're reading this book *because you're worried*. But here's the truth: You cannot *worry* your way to abundance. The truly wealthy do NOT worry. I'm not talking about your 80-year-old neighbor who finally has a net worth of a million dollars after worrying for decades. He's not wealthy in my book. I'm talking about the truly wealthy.

I don't worry. Bill Gates. Warren Buffett. Elon Musk. Jeff Bezos. Jay-Z. They aren't worried. And they have total freedom and massive impacts on billions of lives, but the Millionaire Next Door *is* worried. Because he's obsessed with controlling costs instead of creating wealth.

You probably know I wrote a book called *Be Obsessed or Be Average*. The Millionaire Next Door is obsessed with being average... just so that some day, decades later, they can reach this mythical status called "Millionaire". But an obsession with worrying is NOT what I was talking about in my book. I was talking about becoming obsessed *with success*.

Obsession with worry is the Millionaire Next Door trap. You're trapped into worrying over the wrong thing, just to reach some arbitrary status: "Millionaire Next Door". But you can't worry your way to true wealth. True wealth is the absence of worry. Can you see how solely obsessing over controlling your costs is a losing formula? All of life is just costs — the things you buy with your money and the things you do with your time each minute of every day.

Take out a piece of paper and list out every single thing you did today. Make the list as exhaustive as you can. When you're done, list out what each activity cost you. It might be money... it might be time... it might be your energy... it might be something else you gave up doing. What you'll quickly see is that every day of your life is made up of costs.

There's that old saying, don't sweat the small stuff (and it's all small stuff.) Well, I think it should be — don't sweat the costs (and it's all costs). Because if you re constantly nitpicking and second-guessing costs, you're second-guessing your whole life. Does that sound like the American Dream to you? A life of total and constant worry?

Look, worrying comes naturally to people. I get that. But you should welcome costs. You should want more costs, not less. The trick is being able to properly pay for those costs, which we're going to cover at length. Since all of life is just costs ... Being able to handle more and more costs in your life by getting your money right means you're living more! I'm speaking from experience here. First by watching my mom. And next by living it in my own life.

I remember when I first read *The Millionaire Next Door*, I was attracted by the idea of worrying my way to wealth. I was miseducated like you were. And for the next five years I spent my time trying to worry and save my way to millionaire status. I was pinching pennies. If I traveled, I was sure to stay on a budget at the Holiday Inn. Not only did I not hit my goal. I was miserable along the way. Let's be real, would you rather stay in a Holiday Inn or the Ritz?

Even if *The Millionaire Next Door* worked, you'd still be a millionaire staying in Holiday Inns. Meanwhile, being truly wealthy lets you stay at the luxury hotels and not worry about how much you're spending. I don't want to slowly and gradually save small amounts of money. I don't want to hope that one day, by the time my prostate falls off when I'm 80 years old, if the stock market doesn't go up in flames, I might scavenge just enough money to never enjoy it.

Let me ask you this, are you buying used cars and avoid buying $5 coffee at Starbucks because you believe you're going to save your way to financial freedom? Are you worried about saving enough? If you are, you're right to be worried, because it's not going to happen. This is where *The Millionaire Next Door* doesn't work and why you need to shift your mindset.

I don't want you to be a scared, angry mooch, saving every penny, chasing nickels and losing dollars, while your life passes you by. That's why I say, never ever get your advice from a mere millionaire! Why ask for the view from someone only halfway there. The millionaire is not in the right position to give advice. A person with a million dollars of net worth is not financially secure — they have not financially arrived yet; they only think they have.

Too many people take one of two attitudes towards growing their wealth. They model their financial life after *The Millionaire Next Door*, rather than people who have indestructible, nine- and ten-figure wealth. Or they simply think becoming wealthy is not possible for someone like them. They believe that becoming wealthy is for the lucky sperm club, business owners, gold diggers, lottery winners, athletes, rappers or tech inventors. Both of these are symptoms of the same exact problem — thinking too small.

I used to think too small before emancipating myself. In fact, it's the biggest financial mistake I've made. These are the two biggest financial mistakes I've made in my life — listening to the wrong people and not thinking big enough. There is no shortage of money on this planet, only a shortage of people thinking big enough. The formula doesn't work. It certainly didn't work for my mom. She chose the worry mode of wealth building and paid the price. Millionaires and the super rich come from all walks of life. In fact, just to debunk one of the myths, I'll tell you that four out of five millionaires today work for someone else.

Here's the truth of the matter: The possibility of you becoming wealthy is NOT just a fantasy. The reason most people never create wealth is that they never even consider it a possibility. They're convinced by those close to them to simply be satisfied with whatever their financial situation is.

The other reason is that people fundamentally do not understand money. Very few people know how to get money, even fewer know how to keep it, and almost no one knows how to multiply it. Just look around and you will see signs of this everywhere. The only reason to be obsessed with controlling and cutting costs is that you believe you can't find more money.

Looking back, I realized that my parents were constantly worried about money. It took my dad ten years to firmly secure our family in the middle class, then his heart exploded in his chest. It's my belief that it was his obsession with worrying about "making it" that eventually killed him. Obsessing over controlling his costs cost him everything. After he died, we were right back to worry. My mom didn't know how to get income. She had no income-generating skills that she could use in the marketplace and didn't know where the money would come from. That's what I was surrounded with every day.

If you're reading this right now, you might be living paycheck to paycheck. Or doing better than that but still constantly worried about the future. The question you should ask yourself is how do you get to a place where you are not worried all the time? You need a formula to create wealth... not a formula for getting by.

It doesn't matter who you are. I was broke when I was 25. I hated my job. I had no dad and no money. I knew I wanted to become rich. The Millionaire Next Door route didn't make me rich. Something else freed me from these traps — and I'll be sharing that formula in the following chapters. Thanks to my approach, I now own over 15 companies, control a real estate portfolio worth billions and have helped raise millions of dollars for charities. I know that you can do the same thing if you take the right steps, too. I want to show you exactly what I did to turn my life around and start creating wealth in my life.

But first you need to steer clear of traps like the Millionaire Next Door.

If you want affluence and wealth in your life, you have to change your obsession with worry into an obsession with success. I look for opportunity everywhere I go. You might be seeing scarcity instead of abundance. You're told to eat all your food. To save your money. To be happy with what you have because you're better off than people in other countries. Statements like these might be well intentioned, but they come from a scarcity mindset.

You need to flip that and develop a wealth creation mindset. Start seeing wealth in everything. Instead of looking at someone being frugal and wondering if there is a secret millionaire next door... look for signs of confirmation that there is abundance in the world. Reinforce this by looking at the cars that pass you when you're driving — look at the $70,000 ones... the $80,000 ones... the $120,000 ones. The Lamborghinis, the Ferraris, the Maseratis.

Fill your eyes up with wealth. Be open to seeing how much money exists in the world. Ask yourself, *"Who's a big and abundant thinker in my life?"* Because obsessing over wealth costs just as much as obsessing over worrying. But one obsession leaves you a maybe-miserably-miser ... uhh, I mean, a Millionaire Next Door ... and the other obsession leaves you truly wealthy, with more than enough of what's vital for your life and those you care for.

Think hard to find someone in your life. It could even be a virtual mentor. If you watch my videos or read my material, I can be that person in your life. Let's face it, most of us are surrounded by people with limited thinking because they are worried and have been told their whole life that scarcity is their reality. You have to make a decision that wealth is for you. Someone out there will become wealthy. The question is, will it be you?

When you decide to become wealthy, reinforce that decision daily. Say to yourself, "I am going to create wealth in my life." When you say, *"I don't need money,"* what are you actually saying? You're telling yourself that there's not enough to go around — that you can't get what you need. You're telling yourself you need to primarily focus on your costs. You're hating life because you've given up on it.

Understand that you will need more money to create wealth in your life. Maybe you don't need it now, but your family and church will need it. And you're actually selfish if you commit to being frugal instead of committing to getting more of it. Once you've committed to making more of it, you need to change how you start talking about money.

DON'T TALK LIKE A MISER

How do you talk about money? Are you negative or positive about it? People who obsessively worry about money demean it by saying things like:

- I don't need money
- I don't care about money
- Money doesn't grow on trees
- Money is the root of all evil
- Only greedy people think about money
- Money changes people

How you talk about money will tell me if you've given up on it or are in the game to get it. Listen to what you say, then change it. I would never say money by itself is bad or evil. Money is only a piece of paper. $30,000 is just a bunch of paper notes. How can they be inherently bad? It's like saying sticky notes are bad. That sounds ridiculous, right?

I gave you one million sticky notes right now. Would that change you as a person? What conversation are you having about money with your friends or family? I wasn't allowed to talk about money when I was growing up. It was a private topic. I had to change what I was saying to myself before I could have any kind of financial wealth. How can you expect to get the very things that you need in life if you're hating on them? If you're telling yourself, "I don't have money" or "I never have money", it's going to limit your ability to get it. What's going on in your brain? You probably have a bunch of voices in your head about money.

Remember that 7 out of 10 people that you're surrounded by have problems with money. How you talk about it is how you think about it. How you think determines what you say. What you say determines what you do. Think it — Say it — Do it.

I've raised $200,000,000 for charities and have personally given $10,000,000 of my own money. Was that good or bad? You decide if being able to collect and get that amount of money can help a lot of people. Audit your thoughts and language about money. Take the next 72 hours and monitor what you're saying.

OBSESS OVER INCOME, NOT EXPENSES

If The Millionaire Next Door trap is focusing on cutting your expenses, that builds your worries. The antidote is generating more income, that builds confidence. Worry makes you doubt yourself, which makes you want to cut back even more. Confidence helps you realize wealth is possible, which makes you eventually generate even more income. More income helps you realize wealth.

I can tell you the most important money that I've ever earned was when I went from making $3,000 a month to $4,000. Making that extra $1,000 gave me the confidence and momentum I needed. It taught me that I could do more and that I should do more. Now my single purpose and mission on this planet is to show people like you how to get out of these traps and free to hit the levels of life that I, my wife and kids are enjoying today.

Some people claim that everyone can't have money. They're misers. They think like a millionaire or someone even poorer. They believe there isn't enough money on this planet for everybody. Take it from a billionaire, if you ask billionaires instead of millionaires, you'll realize there are no shortages. People like Mark Cuban, Warren Buffett, Jeff Bezos or Jay-Z will tell you the same thing — just earn more money.

We'll cover how to do that in due course here. I've spent the last 30 years trying to figure out what works, what's duplicable, what's simple and how long it takes to create wealth. I want to educate the planet about wealth and abundance. But first you need to make sure you're thinking big enough. Everything you do and dream needs to go bigger. If you thought you had a good idea, think of it bigger. If you want to throw a party, commit to doing it bigger.

> "You want bigger problems, not little problems. You want bigger amounts of money, not lower costs."

The bigger the challenge, the bigger the interest should be. America is one of the richest countries in the world. If you're not where you want to be, the cold hard fact is, you haven't thought big enough and didn't produce enough each day.

This thinking is hard for those of us who are brought up in poverty or scarcity. Most people would resent bigger problems. Or resent bigger costs. But look at the billionaires of the world instead of the millionaires and what do you see? Billionaires are happier to work more, not less. Millionaires begrudgingly work and dream of retirement. Quit complaining about working. Start bragging about it like a billionaire. Because there's going to be a day when you can't work. You're going to wake up one day and say I wish I could go to work.

Every super successful person that I've studied talks about a 100+ hour workweek. You read stories of billionaires like Bill Gates burning the midnight oil. He'd talk about taking breaks just to grab something to eat and to fall asleep. Otherwise, he was writing code. That's all he did: He wrote code, ate and slept. That's because billionaires are happy to have higher costs, not less. The millionaire next door is trying to avoid and cut costs. Twitter cost Elon Musk $44 billion. Bill Gates' gift to his foundation cost him $20 billion to help people. Each of these guys was happy to pay up. They CHOSE to pay that.

Their goal isn't to minimize their costs. Their goal is how I can have MORE costs to do even more in life. They pay for more things... at higher prices... more often... than almost anyone else on the planet. I can guarantee you The Millionaire Next Door wasn't spending that kind of money or having that kind of impact. He was trapped in the house next door, anonymously worried about his costs and flying under the radar.

Have you ever noticed that? How the people who make the decisions and have the power of choice all seem to be the people with money? They're not trapped, they're free. That's what we're working on here. You don't just want money for the sake of money or for the sake of calling yourself a "millionaire". You want money to be able to have the power of choice!

Which would you rather be? Trapped your whole life for the chance to maybe call yourself a millionaire? Or, truly wealthy as soon as possible, with freedom of choice to positively impact your family, friends, church or community?

Now take a moment to answer the assessment questions before moving on to the next chapter about the misinformation trap.

THE "MILLIONAIRE NEXT DOOR" TRAP ASSESSMENT QUESTIONS:

1. **How worried are you about your expenses?**
    - A. Not at all (1)
    - B. Kind of (2)
    - C. Absolutely (3)

2. **Who is the best person you know of to mentor you about wealth creation?**
    - A. A family member (3)
    - B. A friend (2)
    - C. Uncle Grant (1)

3. **Do you currently believe it's possible for you to become wealthy?**
    - A. Yes, 100% (1)
    - B. Maybe (2)
    - C. No, not currently (3)

TOTAL SCORE:

** These scores will be addressed in Section Four: The Wealth Creation Formula.*

VI.
The "Misinformation" Trap

In this chapter, I'm going to unpack for you the misguided ways of thinking that so many people pick up from their sources of information.

1. **The REAL reason you're not wealthy yet** (and what you can do to change it)
2. **Why your daily cup of coffee is NOT your enemy** ("Bucky's" is not to blame)
3. **The ONLY path to becoming wealthy** (hint: it's not becoming a millionaire. It's becoming a "decamillionaire")

By the end of this chapter, you'll be set to re-wire your brain so it's primed and prepared to accept wealth in all areas of yourself. It's time to get UN-misinformed!

THE REAL REASON YOU DON'T HAVE MONEY

I remember that stinging feeling in my throat as I opened my eyes after my third drug overdose. I was shocked that I was even still alive. As I thought about how I'd ended up there, on a wet floor, stained with my own vomit, the first thing that popped into my head was smoking my very first joint. After that I moved on to pills; first uppers, then downers, then blow, even smoking the rocked-up kind. You name it, I've done it.

Then I remembered the time before that, when I was a young kid who everyone loved — especially my mother. I went from her trustworthy son, someone she adored and admired, to the black sheep of my family. I was definitely at the end of the rope. Five years into my addiction, I tried to get clean. I tried to quit every single day for three years. I just could not quit.

I picked myself up out of the vomit stain. And without even taking time to switch clothes, I headed to see my mom. I already needed another fix, so I slithered into her business, slurring my words, eyes bloodshot, pupils dilated, asking her for money. I was broken and only one person could trigger the desire to UN-break myself.

I came walking in, reeking of drugs, lies and self-loathing, spouting some tale about why I needed money. Then Mom did something she'd never done before. She stopped me and said, "Get out Grant. Don't come here again, I'm done with you." As I stood stunned, believing maybe I'd misheard her, she walked over to the door and held it open. I'll never forget the simultaneous look of anger and hopelessness as she held it open, motioning for me to exit. "Get out and don't come back."

As she closed the door behind me, something inside my soul suddenly switched on. A few days later I was in a treatment center. I needed her to say no. I needed the one person who believed in me most to leave me no option other than to somehow believe in myself. Because that's what the problem had been the whole time. I didn't believe in myself.

I went on to successfully complete the treatment program and immediately in the first 30 days I felt better about myself, but it took some time for me to really start believing in myself. The truth is, no amount of drugs or money or sex or status is going to make it any better. There's no drug in the world that's going to make you more aware, more powerful. Nobody in the history of the world has escaped drugs once it becomes a problem. I would not be where I'm at today if I was still using drugs. I've got an unbelievable life that I would not have. My whole life turned around when I changed the way I thought about myself and got off of drugs.

And that's what this chapter is really about... not drug addiction... the things you may believe based on your history and things you've learned so far. The reason you don't yet have money is because of what you've learned about it. Let that truth sink in a moment. You've been taught wrong! Most people stuck in the middle-class trap are stuck only because they have the wrong belief about themselves and inaccurate information about money and wealth.

If you're having money problems, it's not necessarily because you're stupid, lazy or have the wrong job. It's more likely that the real reason for your struggles related to money is nobody ever showed you what you're capable of... no one ever taught you how to get enough money, how to save enough money, and how to invest it the right way to actually have financial freedom.

I recently did a short documentary about money. It was about how people view money and why they struggle. I went to the streets of Las Vegas for the interviews.

Here are some of the questions, along with the answers I received:

WHAT DID YOUR PARENTS TEACH YOU ABOUT MONEY?

> *"Basically, to save it, but I've never been able to do it."*
> *"How to spend it."*
> *"To save it, and that you have to work hard to get it."*
> *"Be careful with it."*
> *"Spend it wisely."*

None of them were told by their parents to get rich or to concentrate on increasing income first. Everyone was taught by their parents to conserve, protect and view money with a shortage mentality.

WHAT DO YOU SAVE MONEY FOR?

"TO BUY A HOUSE."

I heard this answer over and over. Everyone was brought up to believe that you save money for the purpose of buying that mythological American middle-class dream of owning a home. Like I've talked about several times already in this book, a home will never create wealth for you.

WHAT'S THE BIGGEST MISTAKE YOU'VE MADE WITH MONEY?

"Not saving enough."

I heard this response time and time again. I've said it before and I'll say it again, saving is not your problem, income is your problem. You can't save anything if you don't make anything. People are living paycheck to paycheck, how are they supposed to save? The only way out is to increase your income!

MILLION-DOLLAR MATH

You've been taught your entire life cute little money quotes that are COMPLETELY FALSE. Want proof?

Fill in the blanks from these well-known sayings:

A penny saved is________________.
 A penny earned.

Money doesn't grow on________________.
 Trees.

Money won't make you________________.
 Happy.

You become a robot automatically filling in these sayings, as if they were the truth. But the truth is this: "A penny saved is...", a penny earned? Nope. It's just a penny man, unless you put it into action. "Money doesn't grow on ...", trees? Yes, it does. The paper that physical money is printed on comes from trees and men print as much of it as they desire. "Money won't make you…", happy? OK, but it won't make you sad either, and I'm willing to bet being broke has never made you happy, right?! After all, who has ever woken up in the morning and said, "I'm so happy today that I'm NOT a millionaire!" Literally nobody — EVER!

So, you've been taught wrong — but now what? OK, so we both know that "how to become a millionaire" isn't taught in schools. Isn't it funny that schools teach you "how to read and write"; "how to do math"; "how to know history and geography"; and "how to pass a test", but they never bring up the subject of how to become wealthy? Becoming wealthy seems to be a topic reserved for fantasies, movies, and drunken what-if games.

MOST HAVE COME TO BELIEVE THAT BECOMING A MILLIONAIRE IS FOR THE LUCKY SPERM CLUB, BUSINESS OWNERS, GOLD DIGGERS, LOTTERY WINNERS, ATHLETES, RAPPERS AND INVENTORS.

BUT IT'S NOT TRUE.

Wealthy people come from all walks of life. In fact, just to debunk one of the myths, I'll tell you that four out of five people, technically considered "millionaires", work for someone else. Here's the truth of the matter: The possibility of you becoming wealthy is NOT just a fantasy. The reason most people never become wealthy is that they never even consider it a possibility. They're convinced by the man, the media and the misinformed to simply be satisfied with whatever their financial situation is.

The other reason is that people fundamentally do not understand money. Very few people know how to get money, even fewer know how to keep it and almost no one knows how to multiply it. Just look around and you will see signs of this everywhere. America is one of the wealthiest countries in the world, but...

- 76% of people live paycheck to paycheck
- 50% of Americans have no money for retirement
- 47% of Americans don't have $400 for an emergency

If these statistics were true in a poor country, it would be one thing, but America is considered a wealthy country.

"DON'T DRINK THAT COFFEE"

It's not just schools that have taught you bad ways of thinking about wealth. Turn on the television or go online and you'll see endless, ridiculous financial advice. Financial pundits suggest saving tricks, where your path to "wealth" is finding the lowest price for a product or putting more air in your tires to save gas. This piece of advice always cracks me up: "If you don't drink that coffee, you'll save another $700 a year." You can save $700 a year for the next fifty years and you won't be wealthy, you'll just be old!

Another pundit preaches that "all debt is bad", and that by avoiding debt you will somehow be financially "free". "Never borrow money under any circumstance," the previously bankrupt advisor promotes. He overlooks the reality that almost all wealthy people have used debt to multiply their wealth. Flip the channel and you'll see fancy graphics making the case that you should turn your money over to the boys on Wall Street who, smarter than you, will invest in stocks, bonds, and financial instruments they can't even explain.

Ask your parents for money advice and they will recite their path: get a good job, buy a house, contribute to your 401(k), be grateful you have more than most and pray everything goes right. And ALL that advice... every bit of it is what is keeping you trapped in the flawed mindset of the middle-class American dream. You've received bad financial advice from others your entire life! Most of these people have never created wealth, let alone discovered the formula for doing it.

The first thing you need to do to escape it is pretty simple. Whatever happens though, don't skip over this! It's important and lays the foundation for everything that follows.

DECIDE TO BECOME WEALTHY.

Did you notice that I didn't say, "Decide to become RICH?" I said, "Decide to become WEALTHY." There's a big difference here in mindsets. I don't want you to shoot too low, because the truth is getting rich can happen quickly for anyone. And becoming "rich" IS a step between middle class and becoming wealthy.

The thing is, if you ask most people, they'd say that being a "millionaire" means you're "rich". But the reality is, this isn't 1970; inflation has been eroding the value of the dollar for decades. Quite frankly, a million dollars is not THAT much money anymore. If you want proof of that, let me show you what $1,000,000 can buy you today.

You can get an old, run-down-looking, tiny house in San Diego for $1 million. You get "two" bedrooms with 840 square feet, and it looks like an old barn That's your "millionaire home" today. It probably doesn't exactly fit your idea of living the "lifestyle of the rich and famous", does it?

And that's not only a San Diego thing. It's a New York thing; a Miami thing; a San Francisco thing. In all those cities, a million-dollar home is simply the median price. You need to start thinking beyond a million dollars — to more like $10 million. And, if you need more convincing, let's do the math and I'll show you a million dollars isn't even enough to comfortably retire on.

$10 MILLION IS THE NEW $1 MILLION

If you retire today at 65, with $1 million in cash (after taxes) and no new income, from any source, you'd have to live off of $40,000 a year ($3,250 per month) for the next 25 years before you run out of money. Consider that assisted living can cost up to $76,000 a year and those 25 years are cut to 12, which means you are just about broke at 77. And all this assumes no inflation or critical life events: lawsuits, divorce, college for the kids or — heaven forbid — even more serious situations like cancer, a car accident, a family member in trouble, death of the breadwinner, economic downturn or loss of a job.

I know the idea that "a million dollars isn't enough" may be hard for you to swallow, but your opinion doesn't change the reality: A million dollars is simply not what it used to be. I know firsthand how fast an emergency can devastate a household. My dad died in his peak earning years from heart disease. My mother immediately had to sell the house and manage five kids through college on the death benefits provided by insurance. I watched my mother live in fear every day not knowing how long the money would last.

As I graduated college from McNeese State University in the 1980s, becoming a millionaire was an almost iconic and unachievable status. Today, billionaire Peter Thiel recently suggested that the "single-digit millionaire" can't even afford to access legal defense in America. $1 million is fine if you have just one year left to live. If you have 30+ years left, you've got a problem because you'll be worried about your little pile of depreciating paper running out, so you'll be forced to live frugally, pinching pennies.

To make your money last longer than your clock, you need much more than $1,000,000. You need more zeros than minutes. That's the problem with money — time. If you're in poverty 30 years from now it won't be because you've bought a latte every day, but because you didn't think big enough and didn't produce enough each day.

So my question for you is simple... and this determines everything about your odds of escaping the middle-class trap and creating true wealth: Do you believe $10 million is possible for you? You have to decide that you will become a decamillionaire, and then you must reinforce that decision, over and over. Put a stake in the ground right now: "I am going to become very, very wealthy."

Although some people will judge you for making this decision, just remember that nobody who has created wealth will frown or judge you negatively — they will pat you on the back and say something like, "Great, you can do it and, by the way, you should!" Those who have created wealth understand that creating financial freedom is a worthy adventure. Is it *truly* possible for anyone? Remember, most rich people today are self-made, what's called "first generational," meaning they created their millions without inheriting the money.

And before that little automatic voice in your head says for the millionth time, "I don't want to be wealthy," or, "I just want enough to be happy," you should understand two points:

- Getting wealthy isn't just about you, and
- Limiting yourself financially invalidates your abilities.

Most of us are convinced to settle for basic necessities: clothes, a house, transportation, time off, maybe an upper-management position and some money in the bank. This is the middle-class trap. It is the opposite of the Wealth Creation Formula. It's the Status Quo Formula.

The middle-class trap is for people who settle for "just enough" rather than striving for wealth. The middle-class trap is a compromise and it's selfish. When you compromise your finances, you become unable to help others because you're struggling to simply take care of yourself.

The other part of this is the constant invalidation of you! You are capable of way more than you know, so why set reasonable financial goals? For my entire life, I have had this constant gnawing in me that knows I can do more, achieve more, create more, give more and help more.

But enough of the esoteric and back to the material world. You can earn $80,000 a year or $400,000 a year and still struggle, depending on where you live and your responsibility level. Just because someone makes more money than a person born in some starving village in a third-world country doesn't mean they are much better off. The argument is, "You have a cell phone, internet access, running water and electricity — be grateful." That's code for, "make sense of your situation."

A man once told me, "How do you make sense of insanity? The answer is you don't!" And not having enough money is insane. The idea that someone would only need enough to be "comfortable" or "adequately satisfied" or "have more than others" as a way to justify his or her condition is ridiculous. The middle class is hundreds of millions of people convinced by the man, the media and the misinformed to turn your money over to those smarter than them. "Just settle down in a nice house and be a civil, law-abiding taxpayer who is grateful how much better off you have it than those who have less." All that is designed specifically to reduce your ability to move for the next thirty years.

BECOME A DECAMILLIONAIRE

So, make a decision right now to become a decamillionaire and debunk all the ideas that idolize the mythology of the middle class.

The temporary comfort provided by the house, a "good" school, a couple of BMWs, a 401(k) and two weeks off per year is nothing compared to creating indestructible wealth. You have to make the decision, RIGHT NOW, to drop your small, defensive, take-no-risk thinking. It has never been easier to build wealth, but it is still impossible if you don't change your mind.

There is so much money in the world today and so many ways to create wealth, but it will not happen if you settle. Make the decision right now: "I am going to be a decamillionaire and I am going to help a lot of people in the process."

Making this decision is far more essential than you may realize. Have you ever noticed how the people who make the decisions and have the power of choice all seem to be the people with money? You don't just want money for the sake of money, but to be able to have the power of choice!

I remember at the age of eight, one of my first experiences with money was walking to the local grocery store. I had a quarter in my pocket to spend at the store. I was excited, giddy and I felt powerful. I was walking to the store with my brother fondling my quarter when I dropped it in the street and it rolled into a manhole. I got onto my hands and knees, only to discover my arms were too short to retrieve the quarter. I got up wet, dirty, angry and wanting to cry.

I remember going home and telling my father how I had lost my quarter. My father said to me, "You shouldn't play with money." My grandfather later grabbed me and said, "Son, the problem isn't simply that you lost the quarter; the problem is that it was your only quarter." Since that loss, I have been fascinated with the idea of amassing enough money so no single event or loss would ever cause me to be without.

When it comes to building wealth, you don't need to trust yourself at this point — simply put your trust in someone who has done it. When I first started studying wealthy people, I put my trust in them, because I could not yet trust myself. Trust me to take you to your first million and beyond because I know that if I did it, you can too.

Benjamin Franklin was the first millionaire in America. Now, there are millionaires being made every day — and many of them are becoming decamillionaires. And by failing to prepare for wealth, you are preparing to remain stuck in the middle-class trap. The fact is, creating wealth matters. The decision you make about this will impact your grandchildren. The actions you take today will affect generations of your family. It matters to your kids, your spouse, your parents and your community. Becoming a multimillionaire is your duty.

"THE PERSON WHO CONQUERS THEIR SELF IS GREATER THAN ANY WHO CONQUERS A THOUSAND IN BATTLE."
~ BUDDHA

Can you conquer yourself and become financially free? You are either going to do this thing or you're going to decide the leap is too far. What will it mean for you to become wealthy? What will your contribution to the world be? You will have to be different and do things differently. Wealthy people aren't average people, doing average things.

That's why your decision to become a decamillionaire is your next step to becoming wealthy and escaping the middle-class trap. Start by surrounding yourself with the right people. The way to make more money is to get connected to those that already control money. A network is defined as a group or system of interconnected people or things.

What is your network?

- Immediate Family
- Friends
- Extended Family
- Co-Workers
- Social Media Connections
- What You Are Reading

I don't go to 'work'. I go to my netWORK to increase my Net Worth. You need to improve your network to increase your Net Worth. It's not just about the hustle. You have to have a strategy, a target to hustle toward.

Can you imagine going into a restaurant and telling them, "Give me whatever you've got"? The menu is large, and in life, you can connect with anybody you want to, but don't settle for the grilled cheese when you can get the steak or lobster tail — or both. That's why you've got to get specific: Pick just a couple of people to get information from. If you go to CNN.com and search "oil" you'll get 3 articles that say don't buy oil and 3 that say buy oil. Who will you trust?

It's never been easier to create whatever network you choose and it's also never been easier to have your network contaminated. With so many social reaches through Facebook, Twitter, YouTube, LinkedIn, and endless articles and webinars, it is vital that you control your network to control your net worth.

MORE LIFE COACHES THAN SMARTPHONES

Most of us are brought up middle-class poor and then hold ourselves to the limits and ideas of that group. Getting a mentor to emulate is a success hack of monster proportions. It's what helped me throughout my career to both know what to do and what to avoid doing. What is interesting is I have never met any of my mentors — NEVER. But I feel like I know them, because I dedicated myself to learning everything about them from their first work to their last.

A super-successful person will probably not be able to make time to sit with you. I can be mentored by Mark Cuban without taking his time by reading everything and anything he has written or said. I can study Warren Buffett by simply reading his books and watching interviews. The problem today is that it seems there are more life coaches on the planet than smartphones. Your mentor has to have more horsepower than you do. If they roll up in a Corolla, you have to roll out!

While grabbing a mentor has never been easier, that's good and bad. Easy access means you can get too much information from too many sources resulting in conflict and doubt. Be selective. Immerse yourself in the material I'm presenting in this book. Remember this: If you want to get the most out of your mentor, do what they say, exactly. I get people who adjust and tweak my advice and then end up with something I never advised in the first place. If you change the recipe even a little, you can ruin the dish.

So, what's next? You've probably realized by this point that you've been taught wrong about wealth creation your entire life. Hopefully you're ready to make a big change. You believe becoming wealthy is still possible and you've made the decision to become a decamillionaire. This is just the baseline, NOW you're ready to begin. My first goal for you is for you to lose your millionaire virginity because you're not going to jump from where you are now to $10 million without first crossing $1 million, right?

So, right now, what I want you to do is complete the assessment exercise below. The information you put here will be a vital part of your Wealth Creation Formula in Section Four of this book.

Now take a moment to complete the assessment before moving on to the next chapter about the miseducation trap.

THE "MISINFORMATION" TRAP ASSESSMENT QUESTIONS:

1. **Which of these three things do you believe is holding you back most from becoming wealthy?**
   - A. Your intelligence (3)
   - B. Your charisma/personal appearance (2)
   - C. The misinformation you have received about money (1)

2. **Which of these idioms did you hear frequently growing up?**
   - ☐ "A penny saved is a penny earned." (1)
   - ☐ "Money doesn't grow on trees." (1)
   - ☐ "Money won't make you happy." (1)
   - ☐ "You need a college degree to be successful." (1)
   - ☐ "You have to save money for a rainy day." (1)

3. **What of these five ways of thinking about money did your parents teach you?**
   - ☐ Basically, to save it, but I've never been able to do it. (1)
   - ☐ How to spend it, without thinking about it. (1)
   - ☐ To save it, and that you have to work hard to get it. (1)
   - ☐ Be careful with it. (1)
   - ☐ Spend it wisely. (1)

TOTAL SCORE: ☐

** These scores will be addressed in Section Four: The Wealth Creation Formula.*

Section Three: "ASSET" TRAPS

Section Summary: In this third and final section before we start your personal Wealth Creation Formula, I'm going to dispel the three most common traps related to financial assets. Every single one of these three are so ingrained into the fabric of our society that they'll probably ALL be difficult to let go of. Believe me though, when I tell you, if you want to escape the middle-class trap and start creating wealth, letting go of all three of these is a must!

VII. **The "White Picket Fence" Trap**
I could have written this entire book, just around the trap of single-family home ownership. So many people see owning a home as the pinnacle marker of success and stability. It's not. I'll prove exactly why not in the next chapter.

VIII. **The "Diversification" Trap**
This trap is set by the would-be "Wolves of Wall Street" (yeah, that was a jab!). They want to "diversify" your money for you. Why? Because they have no clue what they're doing either! So, they'll put it into income bonds, small caps, large caps, international bonds, Hong Kong (China), China, Malaysia, blah, blah, blah! And in the end, they make off with the ROI (when there is one) and you are the one with your neck on the chopping block.

IX. **The "Golden Years" Trap**
This trap may be the most insidious of them all. It preys on people in their old age. The bait is the idea

of retirement being a never-ending vacation. It's not — not if you've entrusted your money to those Wall Street Wolves, who will keep you diversified and earning just enough from your retirement investments to stay behind the curve of inflation!

VII. The "White Picket Fence" Trap

Trap #7 is my favorite trap to wake people up about. This trap is designed to trigger your love of home and family, combined with the false belief that purchasing a home will make you rich. SPOILER ALERT — it won't. Read this chapter only if you're ready to find out the truth about...

1. **How the home ownership model was created by the banks** (as a product to help them sell and re-sell marked up money)

2. **Why the wealthy never buy a house** (until they can afford to pay for it in full, without feeling the price)

3. **Why fifth-grade math is all you need to make money with real estate**

The topic I cover in this chapter is without a doubt the topic I am most famous for. My contradictory position on home ownership may disturb you, but it will make you see things differently!

THE NINE-TIME HUSTLE

Before I officially begin, let me make a little disclaimer. I've always loved real estate. I think real property resonates with people, because it's... well, it's REAL! Unfortunately, most people just buy the wrong kind of real estate — a family home. I'm going to call it "unreal" estate. And even though I know what I'm about to say is likely to piss some people off — maybe you — in my opinion it's a selfish decision to own a home, until you reach the level of "wealthy".

To be clear, I'm not saying that most people shouldn't buy a home. I'm saying that NO ONE should buy a home. I know that's the opposite of the American Dream. But the thing is, home ownership as the model currently functions, was not made for people to create wealth. The home ownership model was made by the banks — for the banks to create wealth. They engineered the mortgaged home as a product, specifically designed to sell "marked up" money. Honestly, you can't blame them since it's bad banking to just loan people money with no collateral. That means you need to place a product in between the borrower and the lender — something people can touch and something they will value.

When people start really understanding what I'm telling them about the modern home ownership model, they're like, "Wait Grant, what did you just say?" The fact is the banks can't just lend money for the sake of lending money. They need a reason to loan you money. A business loan is one potential reason, but it's really risky for the bank.

When I was 16 years old, I found out about the fact that every dollar a bank receives, can be lent out up to 9 times. So back in the 50s, the American Dream was invented. Close your eyes for a moment and imagine, if you will, a bunch of bankers sitting around, smoking cigars and sipping bourbon. One fat banker turns to another and says, "We need to lend more money. So, what's the best way to get people to ask us to lend them money?" The other banker says, "Everybody wants a home!" They all grin. "Oh, man, that's pretty good!" "We can't just call it a house. Let's give it a better name." "How about 'The American Dream'?" "Oh, that's rich! And let's tell them, everyone should have one and if not they're a failure!"

Then they got the politicians in on it and it worked so well, they came up with other similar bait to get people asking to borrow money. College degrees and auto loans were two of the other schemes they concocted, "Everyone SHOULD have a proper education!" "Yep! And everyone needs a shiny new car too. Sure, they don't have the money for those things... but they SHOULD have them, because that's the 'American Dream!'" And as they offered free loans for that mandatory college education, insurance, gas prices and tuitions soared!

Hey, look, I like a clever pitch as much as any good salesman does, but not when good people are being sold a big old fat lie! So, I do my best to break people of the spell. But what do they say when I try? They're like: "No, Grant, that's not true. I want to own my home. Why are you crushing everything we've been told our whole life? You're just a bad person." Even now as you're reading this, someone else is reading it too and some of them will write to me after they read this and say, "Can you explain that again?"

No, you should never own one door. And I'm not telling you that because I had a horrible experience with my first single-family home. It's what taught me the lesson though — stay away from single-family homes. And ultimately that lesson is what led to me becoming wealthy. I know, when I say that buying your home is a dumb idea, people think the reason I'm saying it is because I own a bunch of rental property. They think I'm trying to trick people into not owning anything. They're convinced I want people to come rent from me.

OK, you caught me! That's my hustle. Or maybe you should look for the hustle that's really being run on you. Look at the only people who are trying to make sense of a single-family home as an "investment". I'm talking about the ones who are trying to sell you into buying one. I'm not trying to sell anybody on anything other than creating financial freedom for themselves.

There's not one report in the history of this country — 300 million people — of anyone creating financial freedom because they bought a house. You hear those "investment" gurus talking about how great the economy is and how the stock market's going up. "Everything is going to be great over the next hundred years." Right! They're not thinking about the people buying houses when they say that. They're thinking about their rich friends flying Gulfstreams. These are the richest people on the planet. These people don't even talk about the house they bought.

When Donald Trump buys a house, he doesn't buy one. He buys the entire building and he lives in it while collecting rent from everyone else. And I know the everyday person is like, "Well I'm not Donald Trump. I can't do that man. But what I can do is buy a little piece of the American Dream by owning my own home. One day it'll be paid off."

Go fly over Sao Paulo, Brazil. You know what you'll see? So many skyscrapers you can't fit them into a single frame. I actually thought they were all office buildings. They're not though. The skyline of Sao Paolo is littered with residential buildings. Millions of people live in little boxes in the sky, under the false belief that they'll be worth a bunch of money someday. It's not going to happen. It's a trap.

People are making their biggest investment in their home, when they should be making that same investment in themselves or their business, instead of unreal estate. You should invest in yourself first and only businesses that produce immediate cash flow, including real estate other than a single-family home.

And a lot of people recently have asked me, "Grant what about owning a home and renting it out on Airbnb?" I always tell them the truth. Airbnb is the latest thing when it comes to the real estate market. But if you're wondering whether that's a real business or if you're just spinning the wheels, I'll tell you...

Airbnb is a short-term economic opportunity that may do well during an up economy, but it cannot sustain, because all travel and stay demands a good economy. I don't know many people making a lot of money doing it. I do know a lot of people educating people about how to run an Airbnb business and they are making a lot of money doing it.

All that said, when Covid hit in 2020 and the economy started falling apart, the first thing that went was hotels, travel and airlines. People quit traveling. Businesses quit sending their salespeople out on the road. Everything went back home.

When I travel to New York, for instance, I either stay at the Peninsula, the Four Seasons, the Marriott, the Plaza or one of the hotels in the area. But if I don't come to New York for business anymore, because the economy gets crushed, guess what, everybody gets hurt, including the Peninsula, the Four Seasons, the Marriott and the Plaza. Thing is, they've got money to get them through an economic contraction. The

Airbnb guy that depended upon Airbnb travel, all of a sudden that guy gets whacked. He can't get his $80 today. His model is built on half the year. He did the math and he's only got one unit. You're stuck with a business that does not have dependable cash flow and a business is only as valuable as the cash flow is dependable.

Back in 2020, before Covid, a lot of people asked me if a recession was coming. I knew we were already in it. I watched those guys on Wall Street talk about how great the economy was and thought to myself, "For who man? Who's it great for?" At the time, I had 175 employees who worked for me down in Miami. I know eighty or ninety were having trouble, and I take care of my people when it comes to compensation. I pay them fairly, but I can only pay people so much.

The cost of living, mostly in large cities, was so high, even before 2020. The cost of living, after taxes, after renting a place, after the cost of food, transportation and insurance, is ridiculous. And yet, companies weren't paying more money, even though we were experiencing the lowest unemployment that we've had in 50 years maybe since I've been alive.

Wages should have been soaring straight up, but they weren't and they're not today. The rich are getting richer. You're talking about a massive transfer of wealth. So, the question is in always, "Who's got my money?" This is what you should be asking yourself, "Who's got my money?" Not in a form of protest, but from a pissed off standpoint set to start a hunt.

I was 25 years old and I was broke. I had no money, but I got pissed off about it. I'd ask myself, "Who's got my money man? Who's got what I want? Who's got my dream? Who's got my business?" That's what people need to ask themselves today. The wealthy are getting wealthier, because the wealthy play by a different set of rules than everybody else in America. They follow the Wealth Creation Formula.

Meanwhile, people in the middle-class trap are using the Status Quo Formula. They are buying homes and they are buying cars. They are also paying for country club memberships, if they can afford them. They borrow money to send their kids to "good" schools. They save their cash and invest in retirement accounts. That formula keeps them stuck in the middle-class trap.

The wealthy do none of those things. They don't borrow money to go to college. They send their kids to the best college and say, "Hey, don't worry about learning anything. Focus on meeting the Obamas. Make sure you meet the people with the right names." They don't worry about buying houses. They buy businesses. They don't save cash or invest in retirement accounts. They invest in companies. Their priority is to create wealth for themselves and their families. And, like I said earlier, not a single wealthy person you know or will ever meet has built their wealth on the back of the "white picket fence" trap.

Don't get me wrong. I love investing in real estate. It's a major reason I was able to become a self-made millionaire. But I've learned that buying a single-family home to live in isn't a great investment. I realized this in 2004, when I was a newlywed, and bought my dream home in Los Angeles. But as time went by, I wasn't seeing a return on the money or time I put into my house. So, I sold it and used the equity to purchase a few rental properties. Then my family became renters again.

I still support homeownership. Today, I own three homes — two of which I rent out, and the third is my primary residence. But at the end of the day, for most people, owning a home takes money out of their pockets. Here's specifically why I believe buying a house isn't a wise investment, especially not right now, with rising inflation:

1. COSTS EAT UP PROFITS: Let's say you buy a home for $100,000 and put a $5,000 down payment. Then 10 years later you sell the house for $200,000. It looks like you killed it: You turned $5,000 into $100,000, after you pay your mortgage. But you forgot to calculate the cost incurred to own that house:

- 10 years of interest at 6% each year: $60,000
- 10 years of property taxes at 2% each year: $20,000
- Real estate fees of 6%: $6,000
- Total cost before maintenance: $86,000

That leaves you with a net return of $14,000 (or 14%) of that $100,000. Over 10 years, your investment returned 1.4% per year, and we didn't even include the cost of roof, plumbing, paint and other maintenance fees.

A good general rule to keep in mind is that you will spend about 1% of your home's purchase price on maintenance each year, but those fees can be more expensive during times of high inflation.

TIP: DON'T BUY A HOUSE EXPECTING TO MAKE A TRUE PROFIT. INSTEAD, ONLY BUY WHEN YOU HAVE ENOUGH INCOME, WHETHER IT IS PASSIVE OR ACTIVE, TO FUND THE COST OF MORTGAGE, PROPERTY TAXES AND UPKEEP.

2. NO CASH FLOW MAKES YOU DEPENDENT ON THE MARKET: True real estate investments provide you with monthly passive income — cash flow — after all the mortgage payments, property taxes and maintenance. When your home doesn't provide monthly cash flow, its value is always tied to having a homebuyer who is qualified to buy and who likes your home. You pay to live in it while you wait to maybe make a profit. Tough times often benefit the value of rental properties and hurt single-family homeowners. When I go to sell a rental property, I only need to find someone who wants to make a profit, and that's not hard to do.

TIP: ONLY BUY WHEN YOU FIND A TROPHY PROPERTY THAT'S SELLING BELOW ITS VALUE, CAN AFFORD TO PAY IN CASH AND ARE 99% CERTAIN THAT THERE'S A PROFITABLE EXIT DUE TO THE SURROUNDING MARKET.

3. LIMITED TAX BENEFITS COMPARED TO COMMERCIAL REAL ESTATE: For instance, you are limited to how much interest you can write off your home, and you are only allowed a tax exemption of one $250,000 gain on the sale of a single-family home every two years. But when you go from investing in your house to investing in income-producing real estate, the tax benefits skyrocket. While rental income is taxed, there are certain expenses you may deduct on your tax return, including mortgage interest, property taxes, operating expenses, depreciation and repairs.

TIP: TO MAKE PASSIVE INCOME OFF OF REAL ESTATE, INVEST IN RENTAL PROPERTIES WITH FAVORABLE TAX SITUATIONS.

So, when is it a good idea to buy a home? My opinion: Don't buy a home — unless you can afford to waste money. At best, a home is a place to call your own, and it can provide stability. But if your goal is to create wealth, there are so many other options, things like stock market or commercial real estate investing.

I also don't believe that owning a home should be considered as the "American Dream." For the most part, it's simply a place to live — and there are always costs attached.

FIFTH-GRADE MATH

You have to have cash flow to assist you through contraction. My goal is to meet as many people in this planet as possible to see people that are positive people that have more time to create and to be critical, more time to hustle than they have to hate and they want to actually add strategy and techniques that are proven to grow their business so that they can take care of their family in the church.

This is why I don't buy houses. This is what allows me to move. So, I take 15 million dollars, I buy 60 million dollars worth of real estate. 15 million buys 60 million dollars worth of real estate. I'm going to take 300 million dollars this year and I'm going to buy 1.2 billion dollars worth of real estate. To me it's a good deal. I can become a billionaire. I can control a billion dollars worth of assets for 300 million. All I've got to do is figure out how to get 300 million dollars.

This is all the math I needed. I could have learned this in fifth grade. I don't need any algebra or trigonometry or calculus — just simple multiplication. Leverage 300 million dollars worth of cash to buy 1.2 billion dollars worth of real estate in America. That 300 hundred million dollars is going to pay me $18 million dollars a year in cash flow.

I'm going to get paid 1.5 million dollars every month to control 1.2 billion dollars worth of real estate. This is cash flow — the only real currency. The word currency comes from current. If you look it up in the dictionary the word current — it has to move. That 1.2 billion is not moving. That's good too though because you want something that will grow right?

This flow allows me to keep the asset until it appreciates. So, I take 300 million dollars in cash. It's worth less ten years from now. You don't need another math class. It's going down in value. I take the cash, the trash, and I buy concrete, steel and glass, where people live. No office buildings; no WeWork people pitching me WeWork.

I'll never touch WeWorks. Nobody needs that much office space. We don't buy any retail — nothing — no Macy's, no Bloomingdale's. Maybe one day, but not today. These people have to have a place to live. When we buy this asset, it is cash flowing. We know it's going to make 6% in the first year, five to seven percent somewhere in that range.

We should be paid on that deal. This is really important. This is cash flow. It's what will get you through a contraction. You have to have cash flow to assist you through contractions, that you don't have to work for it. This is the money that you hear people talking about when they use the phrase — "make money while you sleep".

THE "WHITE PICKET FENCE" TRAP ASSESSMENT QUESTIONS:

1. **Do you currently make payments on a home you someday hope to own?**
   A. Yes (2)
   B. No (1)

If you answered "No" to the above,
enter total score of "1" on the following page.

2. **If your answer was yes, what is your total mortgage payment?**
   A. Less than $1,000 (1)
   B. Between $1,000 and $5,000 (2)
   C. Between $5,000 and $10,000 (3)
   D. More than $10,000 (4)

3. **What do you pay in interest for that home?**
   A. Less than 5% (1)
   B. Between 5% and 10% (2)
   C. Between 10% and 20% (3)
   D. More than 20% (4)

4. **What is your yearly property tax amount?**
   A. None (1)
   B. Less than $1,000 (2)
   C. Between $1,000 and $10,000 (3)
   D. Between $10,000 and $50,000 (4)
   E. More than $50,000 (5)

5. **What is your average yearly cost for maintenance on that home?**
    A. None (1)
    B. Less than $1,000 (2)
    C. Between $1,000 and $10,000 (3)
    D. Between $10,000 and $50,000 (4)
    E. More than $50,000 (5)

TOTAL SCORE:

* *These scores will be addressed in Section Four: The Wealth Creation Formula.*

VIII.
The "Overdiversification" Trap

Trap #8 is the most counter-intuitive of all the 9 BIG traps. It seems to make a lot of sense that you should invest your money in a way that's spread out, so it's not too risky. The problem is that's not what actually happens in this trap. What actually happens is some Wall Street Wolf winds up spreading your money in too many directions and they get to keep the lion's share of the return. In this chapter you'll discover:

1. **Why Wall Street continues to get so rich** (and you never will)
2. **Why diversifying is not the way to get wealthy** (it's something you do, after you're wealthy)
3. **How Mark Twain nearly lost everything because he didn't understand the principles of diversification**

Like nearly all of the other traps, it's not about NEVER diversifying. It's really all about WHEN. Read on and make sure you're not getting stuck in a way that will have you wind up on the side of the road after working your butt off your whole life.

VIVA LAS DIVERSI-VEGAS!

Diversification is really about lack of commitment, due to fear. If you want to be wealthy, you have to go ALL IN, then build up your wealth to the point where you have enough to invest, then diversify when it can't hurt you. Author Mark Twain went all in on writing. He committed and famously wrote *The Adventures of Tom Sawyer* and was one of the highest-paid authors of the 1800s. But even though success and getting a bit of money sounds good, there is also a danger because you have something to play with. That tempts you to not just diversify, but to speculate.

Twain went from making a bunch of money as an author, to then promptly losing a bunch of money by diversifying AND speculating. If diversification is like Wall Street Roulette... then diversification + speculation is like Russian Wall Street Roulette. Speculating is playing around with your financial life.

Mark Twain's life-changing financial losses came from speculation. Beginning in 1880 Twain spent $300K *(about $7 million in today's dollars)* on investing in the Paige typesetting machine. He thought this device was going to replace human typesetters, and he told the press, *"It can do anything a human could, except drink, swear, and go on strike."*

The problem was the machine never worked that well. As often happens with new technology — it can be buggy and high risk. If anybody knew about the publishing industry, it was Mark Twain. This just goes to prove that even if you know an industry well, it doesn't mean your investment idea is going to work.

He was so overconfident in this little contraption that he spent much of his wife's inheritance in the machine, and even borrowed against the assets of his own publishing company! Twain wasn't finished making bad business deals. Usually, if you know someone making one bad deal, know that it's likely NOT their only one.

Twain lost money on the following:

- An engraving process
- A magnetic telegraph
- A steam pulley
- The Fredonia Watch Company
- Railroad stocks

My friend Mark Cuban says, "diversification is for idiots." I prefer to say, diversification is a middle-class trap. Now I know you, and a lot of other people, are probably going to disagree with me. Like so many other people, you've been sold the idea of diversifying your investments. But it is a trap set for you by Wall Street.

The truth is Wall Street benefits when you diversify. If you have 100 different investments, you need a professional. And that's why the pack of Wall Street wolves has trapped you in the diversification lie. Diversification is the principle that all these big investment funds are based on. It's also why Wall Street continues to get so rich.

You go to a casino to "place lots of little bets" all over. And you know that the house always wins. Why do you think the odds are any different in Wall Street's casino? As long as you keep putting down more and more bets down on their roulette table, you'll continue to lose. Some people might get lucky, but most of the middle class will stay trapped in this sinister trap.

The super rich go all-in on one or two bets and make them work. They don't have a thousand investments — not in the beginning. The super rich go all in on one thing. The railroad barons didn't just buy some railroads... They went out and bought all the railroads they could. When Henry Ford went into cars, he didn't diversify, he went all into cars. Rupert Murdoch didn't just buy one newspaper and then switch niches. He buys all the media outlets he possibly can.

Most super wealthy people go all in on one thing. That's how you make hits. But the middle class is taught what? Put a little money here... and a little money there... and another little bit of money over there. You're told to put dozens of bets out there. And why? Who benefits from 27 investments? Wall Street does.

If you study the wealthiest people — not the person who's trying to sell you on investing in some mutual fund, but the money giants on this planet, like the people who've built the railroads, built the biggest companies or have the best investment track records — they go all in. They don't diversify. They don't spread out and get into six or eight things.

Even some examples of super wealthy people investing on Wall Street can be a trap if you don't have the full context. Take Warren Buffett. At first glance, it might seem like he's diversified. His company, Berkshire Hathaway, owns plenty of different positions in publicly traded companies. He's diversified, right? He's got money in Coca-Cola, Walmart, Wells Fargo, Kraft, Heinz, Apple, Procter & Gamble, American Express and more.

Today, Buffett is to a point of wealth where he can expand and create multiple flows of income. But Warren Buffett didn't start with six or eight or ten or thirty investments. He started out with one thing and made a big bet. After success, he made a second big bet. Then, he made a third big bet.

Why does he diversify like that? There are two reasons: First, because he's got so much damn money now. When your wealth starts expanding, if you want to start diversifying, be my guest. But diversifying is not the way to get wealthy. Second, there were probably a lot of times when he wanted to buy more of any individual company, but there were hurdles to doing it. In those cases, he was forced to diversify, not doing it by choice. But he didn't diversify to get wealthy. I don't want you to diversify. Diversification is NOT part of The Wealth Creation Formula.

WHY DO PEOPLE DIVERSIFY?

Most people diversify because Wall Street and money managers tell you to take the money that you save and diversify. But news flash: Wall Street and money managers don't know what they're doing any more than you do.

So, what do they do? They take a little money and put it in bonds... and take another little bit of your money and put it in aggressive growth stocks... some other sliver of money in small caps... another chunk in large caps... yada, yada, yada. Diversification is based largely on fear. But fear is what prevents people from becoming wealthy in the first place.

People diversify because they're afraid of making mistakes. But if you've diversified your money, you're already making the biggest mistake of all. And if you're making an investment with part of your saved money and you don't know what you're doing... you're already in the diversification trap.

Warren Buffett says: *"Diversification is a protection against ignorance. Diversification is not required if a person knows what they are doing."*

The people who actually make it, make big bets on one thing. Not little bets on seventeen things. Once you get a lot of money then you can diversify. To get money, though, you need to go all in on something. I never diversify investments. I've got the real estate game. I take every cent I make in my business ... and push it all into one real estate deal at a time. I know what I want to invest in and why. And I make sure that investment is rock solid.

But to go all in on something, you need confidence that it's unbreakable. And to have that confidence, you need to have deep knowledge of that one thing. I take all the free money I've got and push it into one deal. You might have heard me say: "Don't be a little bitch." Well, I think diversification is for little bitches. And the reason why is diversification shows a total lack of commitment. It's a crutch to not take responsibility for learning something the proper amount to fully dedicate your hard-earned money toward.

Andrew Carnegie said, "Take all of your eggs and put them in one basket and watch that basket" Carnegie was not a little bitch. He knew steel. And he went all in on steel. Likewise, every wealthy person I know is loaded up into one basket. Until they got so wealthy, they started buying up other baskets. I'm so confident in my one thing — real estate — that when I go all in, I mean I go all in. I'm broke because my money is all in real estate. This means, to pay my bills I have to go get new money to make sure I can keep living. That sort of massive action is true confidence.

But most of the middle class doesn't have the confidence to go all in and watch the basket. They'd rather pass the responsibility off to a money manager and hope in the myth of diversification. Why is it hard for you to have that confidence? The blame also falls on... you guessed it, diversification.

Finish this sentence for me: *"A jack of all trades and a master of______________."*

If you answered, "A jack of all trades and a master of none" you're right. Except, the full quote, from Shakespeare, is: *"a jack of all trades is a master of none, but oftentimes better than a master of one."* Well, guess what? Shakespeare was dead wrong. The irony is, Shakespeare went all in on one thing — playwriting. That's because he knew enough to go all in on one thing.

The truth is: People who diversify their commitments make no commitments at all. And no commitment equals no results. Commitment means devoting yourself completely to something. To be truly great at something — great at investing, great at business, a great spouse, a great friend, a great parent, a great community leader, etc. — you must truly commit. Yet, in so many ways, the middle class is trapped by diversifying their commitments in all areas of their life. Here are some of the areas the middle class diversifies because they lack knowledge, confidence and commitment:

- **Their investments:** We've covered this one. The middle class typically doesn't know where to invest, so they agree to Wall Street's scheme to have them invest everywhere.

- **Their routines:** People have one routine for the weekday, another routine for the weekend, another routine for travel, another routine for holidays. They diversify their routines based on how they feel. Because they're afraid of committing.

- **Their information inputs:** How many times have you heard people say they like to get lots of different opinions? Diversifying your informational inputs is a surefire way to paralyze yourself.

- **Their spouses:** How many households have broken marriages because of a spouse cheating? Or divorce because of money troubles or lack of commitment to supporting each other? How many people are diversifying their spouses in the hopes of not making one big mistake for their whole life?

- **Their skills:** How many people are constantly trying to learn a brand-new skill instead of getting even better at the one that's vital to their income in their primary job?

- **Their plans for the future:** Do you know anyone who makes "Plan Bs?" If so, you have an example of someone who tries to diversify their future out of fear of committing to Plan A.

- **Their children:** How many parents talk about raising a "well-rounded kid?" This is basically diversifying your child's mind because you have no clarity on how to raise them or how to support their natural interests.

The list goes on... Maybe the biggest example of diversifying outside of the investment world is the idea of a side hustle. Side hustles are all the rage today. But they're just a new shade of the same old diversification trap. Maybe you've even considered starting one for some extra cash? There are over 1,000 book results on the topic on Amazon. An infinite scroll of videos on YouTube about side hustles. And over 192,000 "side hustle" news results on Google.

The ideas range from renting out your space and possessions... pet sitting... working events like weddings... freelancing online... doing voiceover or narration work... becoming a notary... online tutoring... delivering groceries. Maybe the most famous hustle is driving for Uber.

Don't get me wrong, working hard is great. And I have nothing but respect for people who have jobs, ambition and the desire to do more and be more. But the problem is, when you do the math, you'll see that side hustles will never make you rich, let alone escape the middle-class trap. If that's your goal, you need a different strategy.

For example, did you know Uber drivers make a median income of about $154 a month? That comes to $1,860 dollars a year, which means that it would take nearly 538 years to make $1 million — $1 million isn't rich, by the way. It isn't that you are not capable of becoming rich, you just aren't going to live that long!

I'm not telling you this to discourage you. I'm telling you this so I can help you put your focus on what will get you the freedom from the middle-class trap you deserve. Most people choosing a side hustle are trying to create wealth for themselves. They're just committing to the wrong formula. When you learn to commit to what matters, you'll become a powerful and unstoppable person. There is nothing wrong with wanting to become unbelievably wealthy. Success is important in order to live a full life, but you need to identify why you want to do it. Those reasons are your purpose.

Having a purpose will change your viewpoint on being successful entirely. It will transform success from an option to a duty, obligation, and responsibility. As long as you see it as an option, you won't be driven enough to fulfill your potential. That's when you'll start to diversify. Commit to your purpose, it's what you need to put your attention on. It is easier to stay committed when you are motivated by more than money.

When you're focusing only on money, that's when you start to think about diversifying from your main job into a side hustle. One online dictionary defines side hustle as: "*a job or occupation that brings in extra money beyond one's regular job and main source of income.*" See how the side hustle is just a different facet of the diversification trap? Instead of placing little, tiny bets with your money, you're placing little, tiny bets with your time. Instead of working more in your current job, you start to cheat on it. You don't commit. Because having a side hustle means you have a "main" hustle you're not concentrating on.

What results would you get if you completely fixated on your main hustle? In my life, I've found that when I commit 100% to any course of action, I have gotten immediate results. When I've diversified, the results were delayed or never happened. I was in and out of sales five years before I decided to fully commit to it as my career. Before I did so, my performance was average at best. It was only once I was fully dedicated and obsessed with learning everything I could about sales, was I able to make income that could propel me towards my purpose.

So, focus on one thing. Having one job or one core investment isn't a bad thing. A job creates money. One rock solid investment niche — like real estate is for me — can make you extremely wealthy. But you have to get great at your one job. When you do, you'll stop hating it or trying to cheat on it with a side gig.

In Section Four of this book, you'll get your Wealth Creation Formula to follow. The plan will help you learn to make money at one thing: money from the job — the surplus — to invest and create a second flow of income. "But wait a second, Grant" you say. "Didn't you just say NOT to diversify. Why are you now telling me to eventually create a second flow of income?" Depending on one income flow is a huge mistake.

What I've told you here is that it's a trap to diversify your *investments*. Your investments are where you place your time, money or energy. But you do definitely want to have multiple flows of income. Investments are not income. Income is what you're living on. When I say income, I'm not just talking about money flow. I'm talking about opportunities as well. You never depend on one flow. I've seen people making $300,000-$450,000 who are easily in the top 1% of all income in the country, have their industry hit and they lose that one income and they're devastated. One income flow got shut down; income that can stop is just being rich for a moment. Real wealth can't be stopped or destroyed.

To create real wealth, you must make investments that will create dependable income streams of flows over long periods of time. I'm going to teach you later when and how to create more flows of income. You don't want to approach this randomly. But for now, I want you to understand the difference between diversifying your investments because you don't know what you're doing... and committing to going down the path of generating multiple flows of income.

Step one on that path is getting in the right frame of mind about the power of going all in on one thing. I want you to understand one space. I want you to get to know everything you possibly can about that one space. It could be the thing you do right now. It might not be. You know one thing about this space — something that can't be destroyed or go away. No matter what happens on this planet, this one investment will appear on this planet to perform for you.

What are examples of things that can't be destroyed? Housing, rental income housing, water, food. Many technologies or gimmicks that are hot in the stock market are here one day and gone the next. Instead, you should go all in on things that cannot be destroyed. But that requires you to know all you can about that one thing.

You know all of Warren Buffett's stock holdings by name because they are a part of everyday life that aren't going away. Coca-Cola was founded in 1892. Warren Buffett owns 9.2% of that multibillion-dollar company. For him it's a sure thing, Coca-Cola isn't going away. He knows what he's doing when he invests in it. When he looks around, he sees people drinking the soda, their billboards and commercials are everywhere. When the economy turns down people still consume Coca-Cola products — it's a sure thing and it can't be disrupted. When Buffett is forced to diversify from Coca-Cola, he's still making sure he's investing in things that are indestructible.

As we continue on your wealth creation journey, you're going to see that there are essentially three steps to wealth:

1. Earn a high income
2. Keep it
3. Multiply it

By the end of the three steps, you want money coming INTO your account from all angles. You don't want to have your money spread OUT of your account everywhere in "little bets." Like most of these traps, you're going to have to learn how to invert the trap to escape. Instead of having diversified bets with your money, you need a solution to creating diversified cash flow streams. You need money gushing on you from all angles. To do that, you're going to have to find one or two spaces you completely understand, that can't be destroyed, and go all in.

In the story about Mark Twain that I started this chapter with, you can see that Twain did well with step #1 but couldn't do step #2 and never even started #3. Later in life, he began to learn and said, *"There are two times in a man's life when he should NOT speculate: when he can't afford it and when he can."* The keyword here is <u>speculate</u>. Most financial analysts today said that Mark Twain's biggest mistake was a lack of diversification — he was putting all his eggs in one basket. But that's not exactly true.

Yes, he went all in on the typesetting contraption... but the problem wasn't him going all in. The problem was *he just went all in on the wrong thing*. Contrary to popular opinion, diversification is NOT a positive thing when it comes to multiplying your money. I put ALL my money into one asset class — and it's making me a billionaire.

It's said that Mark Twain began to suffer depression later in life. Maybe money doesn't make one happy, but not having money didn't make Twain happy either. Nobody is happy to lose their money. The problem is, once you make a big mistake, sometimes you become a coward and stop investing. Twain passed up the biggest money-making opportunity of his life when he considered investing in Alexander Graham Bell's telephone... only to pass on it.

So, it's very important to escape the diversification trap with the right escape plan. Because you're doomed if the trap gets you from the start... but you could still get snapped up escaping, like Twain did, right as you think you're walking away from the trap scot-free.

The key takeaway right now is that you should start rejecting the idea of diversification in your investment life. You should be building up your knowledge around ONE sure thing. Each investment you make must be like this. You must know it's a sure thing and if it isn't don't play around and gamble with it.

Figure out one space that you understand everything there is to know about and you know for sure, without a doubt that it can't be destroyed and protect that one investment. Find the thing you love and understand and go all in on it. You've been told to invest in little pieces, here and there and to diversify your portfolio — but this is all wrong.

This is a part of the system that holds people back from creating real wealth and traps them in the middle class. You don't want to start with little and end up with little. You want to make huge moves and for that you need to make huge investments. You need to know what you're doing with what you invest in. That's how people become wealthy, not by tiptoeing in with $100 investments all over the place.

THE "OVERDIVERSIFICATION" TRAP ASSESSMENT QUESTIONS:

1. Are you currently investing across asset classes?

A. Yes (2)
B. No (1)

2. How many asset classes are you invested in?

A. None (1)
B. 1 (2)
C. 2-3 (3)
D. More than 3 (4)
E. I don't know (5)

3. What is your risk-adjusted rate of return on your current investments?

A. More than 20% (1)
B. Between 10% and 20% (2)
C. Between 5% and 10% (3)
D. Less than 5% (4)
E. I don't know (5)

TOTAL SCORE:

** These scores will be addressed in Section Four: The Wealth Creation Formula.*

IX.
The "Golden Years" Trap

This ninth and final middle-class trap can be seen as an extension of the previous trap "Overdiversification". It's really more specific than that though. This final chapter is about the "Golden Years" Trap — the magical time of "endless vacation". This one is sneakier than a snake wearing slippers. You need to pay close attention to this chapter because you're about to see...

1. **Why the best-case scenario retirement is really all that great**

2. **How you think about lunch says everything about how you think about the idea of retirement**

3. **What you should do instead of letting retirement send you to an early grave**

This final chapter about the nine biggest middle-class traps is the cherry on top of the whole hoax, before you head into Section 4, where you'll develop your Wealth Creation Formula to escape the middle class and attain the freedom you want. You want to really understand this common trap and steer clear of it!

THE ENDLESS "VACATION"

I was having a discussion with a client and his wife, let's call him "Jim", so I don't reveal anything personal. It was Autumn of 2018, and after years of working, Jim's wife "Maggie" told him that he could retire. They'd been saving for years and they could afford it. Jim never really liked his job, especially the 40-mile daily commute.

The day he retired, Jim and Maggie started a 4-day drive to their retirement spot in Arizona. Almost immediately, Jim felt completely lost, a fish out of water, (Maggie used that term, not Jim). He missed their adult children, who still lived only a few miles from where they were raised. He wasn't interested in any activities, like golf or tennis. The community in Arizona offered so many things, but he just didn't show any interest.

After a couple of months, Maggie saw that Jim was in a deep funk. The lack of structure his job offered, along with missing their children made every day hard to bear. She even bought him 2 books on retirement, but nothing helped.

So, after many hours of discussion, Jim and Maggie sold their retirement home in Arizona. And worst of all, Jim is wracked with guilt over giving up the house. Maggie loved it. It was probably the only thing she had ever truly wished for in almost 40 years of marriage. Jim feels like he took it away from her because HE couldn't cope with retirement.

Now, I don't share that story as a downer. I tell you because the "Golden Years" trap is the sneakiest of them all. It prays on the hopes and dreams of people in their final chapters of life. And whereas Jim and Maggie's story is "best-case scenario", there's an even bigger group of people who never even get to the point where they realize what a sham the idea of "retirement" actually is.

There's so much misinformation about retirement, and assets related to it, that it's no wonder most people never create real wealth. I know people who are so "save for a rainy day" people, who won't buy anything if it isn't on sale. Most of them are still broke because they don't understand how to produce income, rather than "saving" their way toward their "golden years".

They spend their entire life thinking money is scarce, when in reality, it's just a currency printed by men. On the other hand, I also know people who know how to produce a ton of income but never learn how to manage it. So, they end up with none of it.

While most of us know that money isn't the only element of happiness, we know that it is "an" element of it. A financial plan is way different than a budget. It's the entry point to wealth creation. Kind of like a road map for managing your income. The first step is to figure out how much money you currently spend. After that you want to figure out how much money you actually need to bring in every month in order to get everything you want to accomplish.

Accounting lesson time: I don't want to get too technical, but the important word you need to know here is "solvency". It's the ability to meet long-term fixed expenses and accomplish long-term growth. In other words, the better your solvency, the better off you are financially. When you're insolvent, it means you can't operate. A lot of people mistake solvency for "profitability", which is your ability to earn a profit.

But you can actually be profitable without being solvent. Where most people fail with financial planning is they never create a plan that makes them solvent. They spend most of their time on the budget portion: car payments, mortgage, credit cards, gas/electric bills, other utilities, insurance, food, restaurants, entertainment, dental and medical bills, etc. Then they completely disregard the more important stuff. A true financial plan should clearly state your monetary goals. You've got to outline exactly how you're going to create surpluses of money, what to do with the surpluses, and how to manage and invest that money.

A plan means you're doing something to make things happen; it's not just talking about what's been done already. That's a budget. Clipping coupons, saving money, cutting back and anything to do with controlling expenses is all about a budget. A financial plan focuses on wealth creation.

The biggest reason a lot of people never seem to have enough money is that they focus their attention on a budget instead of a plan. You've got to spend time thinking about how much money you actually need. And remember there is no shortage of money on Earth. What there's a shortage of is planning, motivation, guts and follow-through.

Lucky you though, because in the next section you're going to get a chance to develop your very own, personalized Wealth Creation plan to help you escape the middle-class trap — in particular the devious "Golden Years" trap.

See, your current lack of wealth doesn't have anything to do with how much money exists. Your ability to create wealth is completely based on how well you understand the way money works and on whether you're motivated to make it work.

TACOS AND RETIREMENT

So, here's a retirement-related continuation of the topic of "diversification" from the last chapter. Someone once asked me, "Do you know Dave Ramsey?" I don't. I know what he teaches, and I'd love to meet him and get to know him. Imagine Dave Ramsey and me in the same environment. It would be freaking awesome!

Dave would say, "You need to save for retirement and get prepared for the day of reckoning." You know, like your parents used to tell you, "A penny saved is a penny earned." and "Save for a rainy day." But the reality is they should have inverted the whole thing. What I mean is, they told you about the bottom half of the financial statement, not the top half. They didn't teach anything about making money.

If you've never been taught how to make money, being taught how to save it is kind of pointless. And honestly, that's why most people never have any money until they're too old to use it. The average American, between the age of 55 and 64, has just $104K in their retirement account. Maybe that sounds like a lot, but $104K only translates to $300 a month that they can spend. Go to Whole Foods, get three bags of groceries and you're broke.

You've been taught to start saving for retirement early. The idea is that the earlier you start, the safer you'll be. The problem is that's not true. When you're 20 years old you have no clue what to invest in. I know people 50 years old who have no clue what to invest in. And because of that, the next thing you're told is to send what you've saved to people you don't know and they'll invest it for you. And, oh yeah, by the way, those people you don't know are going to do a thing called "diversify" for you.

And why do they want to "diversify" your money for you? Because they have no clue what they're doing either! So, they'll put it into income bonds, small caps, large caps, international bonds, Hong Kong (China), China, Malaysia, blah, blah, blah! Translation: "We're going to 'diversify' all the way around the world to avoid money-losing mistakes.

The best example I can give that explains the big flaw of this way of thinking comes down to tacos. And you may be asking, "But Uncle G, what the hell do tacos have to do with diversification?" Great question! I'm glad you asked. When my staff orders lunch for me, it's not "diversified". See, I know what my desired outcome is when it comes to lunch. I want low carbs, high protein and a little heat. That way I can have energy to make money, NOT save it.

Now, if my staff doesn't know what I want, maybe they'd order fish and steak and vegan tofu and chicken soup. And I would have so much food it would be wasteful. For a meal to really be good — I'm talking about getting an ROI on lunch, it can't be a freaking random, mixed-up buffet. This ain't Thanksgiving at Uncle Grant's! I know exactly what I want, "Hey man, give me some tacos!"

The problem is, we're not taught how to do the one thing that matters when it comes to being able to retire if you ever want to make freakin' money! The question isn't, "How do I save money for a rainy day?", it's "How do you make so much money that you've got to start figuring out places to get rid of it?" That's the way you need to think about retirement. You want to make so much freaking money that the spillage will take care of you in retirement.

MAKE MONEY SONNY

The average life expectancy in America is 84 years old. The average desired age of retirement is 62. You do the math. Imagine you're 62 years old; you've just retired after working your whole life; and you've got $104K put away. Now you've got twenty-two years left to live and only $104K. That's only $393 a month to live off of. And let's say you're lucky enough to get Social Security. The average Social Security check is about $1,341. So, you've got $1,734 a month, which actually puts you in the top ten percent.

You've got $1,734 to spend every month. And maybe that doesn't sound too bad. Here's the thing though: the average expenses for a person this age is $3,350 a month. That means you're in the hole $1,600 every month, in the richest country in the world! And this is all because your mama, your daddy and Dave Ramsey got you believing that "a penny saved is a penny earned." Nonsense. They told you to "Start saving early and diversify." If you're listening to what they told you, it explains the trap you're in.

Not a single person I've met has ever told me, "My Momma told me to make a boatload of money" or "My Daddy said, the only thing you need to know about money, Sonny, is that you need to make truckloads of it! Make so much freaking money you don't know where to put it!"

No. What they tell you instead is, "Start early; scrimp and save; put your money toward things like a family home, a college degree and a 401(k). More people have been killed by these three ideas than all the terrorism on the planet. You become a prisoner. You can never even leave. They've sold this golden combo to hundreds of millions of people.

Way back before the collapse of 2008-2009, the Clinton administration lowered the requirements associated with ownership. All of the sudden the floodgates burst open. Everyone could do it. They were setting things up for collapse. Home ownership is the Venus flytrap of wealth. College is a prison. And the 401(k) is probably one of the greatest scams on the American public in history.

Why do people fall for it? The 401(k) was created by Wall Street. It was sold to politicians, who were told, "We will support your campaign if you can get this thing pulled off. Let's spin a story to the middle class and say, 'Everybody should start saving young. Put away a little bit every month.'" This whole story wasn't built for you. It was built for Wall Street, and I can prove it.

I started my real estate investing fund and in order to let people invest, there are rules that make sense. You have to be an accredited earner and, in order to invest in the deal, you have to earn at least $200K per year for two years in a row. Either that, or you have to have a one-million-dollar net worth. That is only four or five percent of the entire population.

I don't want somebody who only has $50 a month do the deal. Why? Because they're not good for it and because Wall Street already has a stranglehold on that group anyway. They want people to start giving them $50 a month at 18 years old while working at Starbucks. "Hey coffee barista, we're going to take $50 out of your check. We're gonna match it with fifty! We're gonna do up to $3K. And we're going to take care of you little buddy!"

What they leave out of the story is, "Oh, and by the way, we're going to trap it for the next 30 or 40 years." That's exactly what financial markets do. They're very complicated and abstract. So complicated in fact there's over $2.8 trillion invested in 401(k). And you can't get the money out without being penalized.

I'm telling you, the whole thing is a scam! You can be wiped out overnight. When you hear your parents say, "Save money. Save money. Save money! Buy a house, a new car, and put money into a retirement fund. You'll be so much better off than other people." Just realize that you're hearing that from people who are financially indoctrinated. Maybe they'll end up retired, with a $300K house. Maybe it will be paid for and they'll plateau for about thirty years; one vacation per year, clipping coupons; with a couple hundred grand in the bank. "We got a free buffet every night and two free breakfasts at the Holiday Inn. We have one million points with Visa and we're using them." What you've got to understand is that this person has basically settled for the bottom half of the financial statement.

DON'T SETTLE FOR THE BOTTOM HALF OF THE FINANCIAL STATEMENT.

I was recently talking with a married couple about their financial statement. As I was going through it, I told them, "You only need to worry about these top two inches — nothing else. If you get the top two inches to be fat enough, with a big enough surplus, you don't need to worry about "retirement." 65% of people in the USA, the richest country on the planet, rely on Social Security for retirement. And these are the people who supposedly "have it made." Look, if "having it made" means a $104,000 in a retirement account, that you can't get to before you're 62, without being penalized, then you and I just have a different definition of "having it made."

What if you need that money earlier? The fact is you were never in control of it you were never in charge of it. They "diversified" it for you. They put it in a bunch of places and that's why it never grew, because the people that actually make it are the people that make big bets on one thing not 17 things — PERIOD. Diversification is a thing you should do, but NOT until you get a significant amount of money. And you need to KNOW what your "critical mass" number is. I'll tell you more about that in Section 4, the final section of this book. That's where you're going to get your Wealth Creation Plan.

Once you're 100% clear what your critical mass number is, you can diversify. To make serious money though, you need to go all-in on something. That's why my main business is real estate. All my other businesses support that. I take all the money from my other businesses, which are all similar. They all kind of run together, and then I take all that extra money and I dump it into my real estate business. Then I wait it out for 10, 15, maybe 20 years, but it ALL pays me as I go.

I've got a house here. I've got a place there. There's money everywhere. That's where you want to be in retirement and you never really need to retire at all. You want to be in the position where there's money everywhere. You don't want to be barely getting by on Social Security, with 1,300 bucks a month, just scraping by. I hope this makes sense to you.

Focus on making money, not saving it. If you've got 10 grand right now, you don't have real money. Just admit it — you're broke. If you have 30 grand, admit it — you're broke. If you got 60 grand in your bank for your business account, admit it — you're broke. Quit acting like that's money, like you're going to hold on to it, like you're going to keep it. Like it's going to be something one day. No, it's not. You have to know what your critical mass number is and spend that money. Invest it in a way that actually means something, in a way that can actually become something significant.

And maybe you're saying, "Saving? I'm not really looking for advice on saving from you Grant. I usually look to you for my financial advice because I follow your sales strategies." Yeah, I know. And that's where you're thinking wrong. My friend had an uncle, his uncle John did really well and everybody in his family thought Uncle John was the man! Uncle John was the guy that did well. He sold stock in a company. His company went public and made him some money. He took that money and bought section 8 housing. Everybody thought he was the freaking man! And he is, based on everybody else's position. You understand? That's the problem.

You have to decide where you're going to get your advice. If you want a couple hundred grand in a retirement account, all I'm saying here is you have to be willing to do the math on the couple hundred grand. The reality is, when you get to 64, you're going to be sweating it every day. Worried whether or not you have enough. And I'm telling you before you get there, that's not enough. What that means is freaking fear for 22 years! There's no real need to "retire" anyway, when you're doing things you enjoy. It's the stress that most people are really trying to "retire" from.

WINNERS NEVER QUIT

Aside from the fact that winners don't quit, there are three big reasons I won't retire and you shouldn't either. I've lost count of how many times people have asked me "Grant, with all you've done and all you have, when are you going to retire and just enjoy life?" I've been enjoying life for over 30 years and I plan to keep right on enjoying it.

Even after all this time and all that I've done, I still wake up every morning just as excited as ever about what the day will bring. New projects, different challenges, the chance to help someone, you name it. In my life and my business, there's no such thing as a typical day. With possibility and potential around every corner, retiring is the last thing on my mind.

REASON #1 NOT TO RETIRE: ENOUGH IS NEVER ENOUGH: Ever see a sports team quit a game because they're so far ahead they think they can't lose? Of course not. It doesn't happen on the field or the court and it doesn't happen in my business. In fact, as far as I'm concerned, the game never ends. I'll just keep on scoring points which, in my case, means making money and helping others do the same.

REASON #2 NOT TO RETIRE: COMPLACENCY IS DEATH: Everyone is so focused on the doom and gloom that they can't see the opportunities popping up all over the place. Right now, real estate alone is a one-way ticket to increased wealth. Then there are so many other needs created by this crisis just waiting to be fulfilled. Businesses that are forward-thinking and agile like mine can adapt and turn adversity into advantage.

REASON #3 NOT TO RETIRE: EXPANSION IS SURVIVAL: I lost my father when I was 10 years old. My family and I were left with almost nothing. I painfully learned that anything can happen. I don't ever want my wife or my children to have to worry so I'm going to provide for them as long as I can. Then there's the family I've created at Cardone Enterprises. I know I'm going to have to pass the torch one day. When that happens, I want to make sure they're in the best shape possible to carry on what I started.

We all get one shot at life, so we have to take our best one. Anything less is a disservice to our community, our coworkers, our family and ourselves. I'm certainly proud of everything I've accomplished both in my businesses and my life but I'm far from done. In fact, I'll get out when I get knocked out and I promise you that's not happening anytime soon.

THE "GOLDEN YEARS" TRAP ASSESSMENT QUESTIONS:

1. **Are you currently saving for retirement?**
   A. Yes (2)
   B. No (1)

2. **What are you currently doing?**
   - ☐ Saving as much as you can for retirement (1)
   - ☐ Saving as early as possible for retirement (1)
   - ☐ Opening retirement accounts (1)
   - ☐ Trusting banks and institutions with your money (1)

3. **Do you see yourself as someone who can actually enjoy the "retired" life?**
   A. Yes (2)
   B. No (1)

TOTAL SCORE: ______

* *These scores will be addressed in Section Four: The Wealth Creation Formula.*

Section Four: THE WEALTH CREATION FORMULA

Section Summary: In this final section, it's time for the payoff. This is where you develop your Wealth Creation Plan. In this section I'm going to walk you through the three phases of wealth creation. That's your path out of the middle-class trap and onto creating lasting wealth for you and your family. You're about to understand wealth and money (there is a difference between those two) using a process that took me over three decades to develop and perfect.

I spent five years getting an accounting degree, because I wanted to understand money. Once I got my degree, the truth is, I really still knew nothing about money. The one big thing I did get out of my degree was an understanding of assets versus liabilities and how to track their effect on the bottom line. So that's where we're going to start.

What you'll see in this section is over 30 years of what I've learned about how money really works and how to escape the middle-class trap by increasing your wealth. I'll show you how to build wealth in all areas of your life, including money, notoriety, health and relationships. You're about to discover precisely how to create multiple flows of wealth in those areas and how to sustain it. Your Wealth Creation Plan is broken up into three major phases:

1. **The Earned Income Phase** - which gets you headed quickly away from poor (a.k.a. "middle class")

by focusing on making the most out of the source of your earned income, your job!

2. **The Investment Income Phase** - where you create multiple passive income streams that will significantly up your cash flow by investing what you've set aside in the first phase.

3. **The Wealth Scaling Phase** - in this phase you're focused on bigger deals, plus human and infrastructure assets that will take you from just "rich" to truly "wealth".

If you hear that dinging sound, it's your captain, Uncle G, mashing the seat belt button up here in the cockpit. I'm just reminding you to strap yourselves in. We're about to land this plane and things are going to get bumpy. The landing gear is coming down, the flaps are going up and right now it's time for...

X.
The Big Payoff

There are three steps before you hit your first critical mass and begin to invest, then create multiple income flows:

1. **Step #1: Create Income**

2. **Step #2: Increase Income**

3. **Step #3: Save (Set It All Aside)**

These three steps are the "skeleton" of your Wealth Creation Formula. They're specifically designed to set up your framework for becoming rich, then wealthy. All along the way though, you're doing much more than just gaining money and material possessions. You're actually developing the traits required to go from middle class to rich, to wealthy.

THE ONLY TWO COLUMNS THAT MATTER!

This book and the Wealth Creation Formula that it helps you develop aren't some "side" project for me. This is the fulfillment of the promise I made to my Mom after we lost my father. My Dad was under tremendous amounts of stress and pressure, doing his best to take care of his wife and five children, as he was building himself into the middle class. At age 16, I told my Mom, "I'm going to be rich one day and I'm going to help a lot of people."

I realized later in life that the exact people I was trying to help were my mother and my father — people like them anyway. I wanted to help people trapped in a hoax that they can't see because they're too close to it. Overall, I can honestly say I've fulfilled both parts of that promise. I am in fact wealthy and I've already helped millions of people, but I'm not done yet. Here, in this book, specifically in this final section, I've created a comprehensive system. It combines all my best methods and models into a single, very simple solution. So, let me explain why I decided to call it the Wealth Creation Formula.

When you're "escaping" one situation, the goal is usually to break free of whatever is trapping you, and move on to something or someplace else, right? In my mind, when you're escaping the middle-class trap, which it really being POOR, your destination is simple — to become WEALTHY. So, the goal of riding on the Middle-Class Underground Railroad is to take you from "poor" (even if it's poor middle class) to being "rich" all the way through to becoming truly "wealthy".

And you might wonder, "Wait Uncle Grant, I'm good with just being rich. Why are you talking about it like it's different from being wealthy?" There's actually a huge difference between getting rich and being wealthy. I want to teach you to get rich, of course. You actually have to, on your way to becoming wealthy. But the truth is, with a bit of luck, nearly anyone can get rich quick. Believe me when I tell you, though, that nobody gets wealthy quickly. My goal is to teach you how to become truly and irrevocably "wealthy".

Making a lot of money is one thing — creating wealth is something entirely different. Wealth is more than just money or material possessions. It's the abundance of something in such surplus, that no condition can destroy it. It's abundant — you can't get rid of all of it. There's so much of it that no matter what happens in the world around you, it can't go away.

So, before we get started, let's define what "wealthy" means. When I say "wealthy", most people think of cars, houses, boats, tennis courts and country clubs. But wealth is not in any way limited to material possessions. In fact, if you look up the definition of the root word "wealth", it's defined as an abundance of something valuable.

Synonyms include words like affluence, riches or fortune. So, that could mean cars, houses or boats. But it could also mean a plentiful supply of any valuable resource. Like a wealth of knowledge or wisdom.

The word 'wealth' comes from the old English 'weal', which means to 'well' or to be in a state of 'wellbeing'. Back in the day, it actually meant to be well — in a health-related sense. So, that seems to imply that if you don't have wealth, you're not well. All that in mind, the Wealth Creation Formula is a method for going from poor to wealthy, by creating an abundance of anything valuable.

As an example, even though I'm a multimillionaire, with numerous assets and a good millions of fans, the area that I am wealthiest in is not money, property or fame — it's friends. I can pick up a phone or post something and say, "I need help." and someone will be there.

What I'm going to share with you here is what you should work to create wealth in any area of your life — friends, fans and of course financial wealth — M-O-N-E-Y. So, let's start there. There are only a few ways to create financial wealth.

The Three Ways to Get Money (legally):

1. Earning — you earn it directly, in other words a j-o-b
2. Investing — you invest in something and get a positive return; earned income from the investment
3. Inheritance — somebody passes it on to you, usually a family member, typically after they die

And you may say, "But Grant, I'm never going to inherit anything." Trust me, whether you realize it or not, you've already inherited a lot. Some of it is assets, a tremendous amount of wealth. But some of it is liabilities, things you need to get rid of. If you were poor middle class like me, your inheritance probably includes a lot of liabilities. You're stuck with the ideas of the poor and the middle class.

And that's really what the Wealth Creation Formula is about, your assets or liabilities and when to focus on which ones. If you really want to create wealth and escape the middle-class trap, you've got to truly understand one key thing. At all points in your Wealth Creation process, you have to be clear on what your assets and liabilities are and which ones to focus on.

So, let me talk about "assets" and "liabilities" and what those terms really mean. In this list below, you can see all the conventional kinds of assets and liabilities. There are the tangible ones, both liquid and fixed, like: cash, accounts receivable and inventory. Then you've got your intangible assets, where the conventional ones are things like patents, copyrights and trademarks.

But there are some other intangible assets or liabilities that you should be thinking about too. These are things that don't go on an official accounting ledger. Things like your relationships, your skills and your beliefs.

TANGIBLE ASSETS/LIABILITIES:

> **Liquid:** Cash, Accounts Receivable, Inventory, Securities
>
> **Fixed:** Homes, Buildings, Land, Equipment

INTANGIBLE ASSETS/LIABILITIES:

> **Personal:** Knowledge, Skills, Beliefs, Relationship (Reputation, Network, Personal Brand)
>
> **Non-personal:** IP (Patents, Copyrights, Trademarks, Trade Secrets, Licenses & Permits) Goodwill (Company Brand / Attention)

YOU, ASSET OR LIABILITY?

I've spent the last 30 plus years doing my best to be honest with myself, so I become an asset, not an "ass". In other words, I look for ways to become more of an asset than a liability to myself, my family and the people who love me. We all generally understand that if you have more liabilities than assets, you've got long-term issues. And this book is about finances – it's about money – but there are more than just financial assets and liabilities.

I mean, sure, you want to ask yourself, "Do I have cash? Do I have a house? Is a house an asset or a liability?" kind of depends, doesn't it? "Do I have stocks? Do I have things like trade secrets or royalties?" But there are some other things that should be on your assets and liabilities list. How about, "Do I have good health or high energy? Do I have quality relationships? What are my friends like? Do I have real friends or are my friends actually liabilities?"

And most importantly, "What about me?", meaning you, yourself? Are you currently an asset or a liability? How do you view yourself and what are your limiting beliefs? For me, when I was first beginning to grow in sales, it took me a long time to understand that I had limiting beliefs. That was especially true when I started making $80-$90K a year in sales.

This was years ago. $90K was the equivalent of around $270K today and I was earning that in an industry where the top producers were earning $40K. The limiting beliefs I had at that time, and then even when I was making a million dollars a year, were the really sneaky ones.

See, when you're not making good money, it's clear you've got limiting beliefs. When you're only making $30K a year, and that's all you can make — no matter how good you are; no matter how much you smile; no matter how much service you provide; no matter how early you start or how late you stay — when you still make $30K, you know there's a limiting belief. Everything would indicate you should be paid more.

When you're making a million dollars a year, on the other hand, you start thinking to yourself, "I don't have any limiting beliefs." So, the way to handle that is you need to study people who've created massive amounts of wealth. I'm talking about people who are not just earning money but keeping money and multiplying it. This is what the great salespeople don't usually do.

I know great salespeople who have never figured out how to multiply their money. I know salespeople who are better at sales than me, but they're still broke. And they're broke because they made their money and didn't know how to keep it, or they kept it and didn't know how to turn it into more.

How much you earn is a limiting belief, but how and where you keep it are even more so. If you have money in the bank or equity in your house or if you have a retirement account, you have a limiting belief about money.

Maybe you have equity in your home, waiting to pay it off after 30 years, like The "White Picket Fence" Trap. Or maybe you're saving for a "rainy day" like I just talked about in The "Golden Years" Trap. No high-performance person needs to worry about "rainy days" or paying their house off. You should rent where you live and own stuff that other people pay you for. Just rent where you live and be mobile.

I'm talking about how you save money; how you spend money; how you invest money; and how you manage diversification. That's also a limiting belief. I know a lot of people recommend diversification, especially those "wall streeters", because they benefit from you diversifying the most. They constantly remind you that you don't want to put all your eggs in one basket.

The thing is, if you study the super wealthy, they never lived by that rule. They took stakes once they got super rich, then they diversified.

APOLOGIES IN ADVANCE

I know I'm going to upset some people with how I think about relationships as assets and liabilities. But the thing is, I tried so hard to be everybody's friend when I was a kid that I ended up not being a friend of myself. I sold myself out so hard that I became a liability to myself.

Look at the people in your life: your friends, your family, your relatives, your colleagues, your partners, the people you collaborate with. I've collaborated with people I put on my stage, who've blown up and become famous, because I've helped them get a bunch of attention. And next thing you know, I'll post something on social media and watch them ignore it because they don't want to make time or because it might make them look bad. That person is not an asset.

Your money is going to be attached to the people in your life. There is no way around this truth. If you have good people around, you've got a better chance of creating wealth. If you have bad people around you, the opposite is true. You'll end up buying stuff you don't need, trying to please people you don't need, who'll drag you to places you don't need to be. We're talking about relationships, the people in your life. This is where you're ultimately going to get your money, so you've got to get this part right — the people in your life, are they assets or liabilities?

Some "friends" will tell you you're fine, even when you're not fine. These are either people who never were real friends or they're friends who've become liabilities. People are either for you or against you. There's no grey. It's black or white. Your friends are either assets or they're liabilities. There is nothing in between. But, how do you know the difference? You watch their actions and the effects of their actions on you and your ability to create wealth.

It doesn't mean they're trying to intentionally hurt you. But even more dangerous than the friend who's an intentional liability, is the "friend" who's unintentionally a liability. They don't even know. You could sit there and tell that person over and over that they're working against you and they'd be like, "What do you mean? I love you. I support you. I do all kinds of things for you."

And then you open up your Instagram or Facebook and see that they've liked Jamie Foxx's or Mike Tyson's or Tony Robbins' posts, but they didn't have time to like yours. They're going to say, "Man I didn't have time. I didn't see it." It doesn't even matter to me. I don't even know why they're defending. I don't care whether someone likes my damn post or not. What I do care about is whether someone is my friend — are they in the asset column or the liability column?

There's no need to convince me. Their actions tell me everything I need to know who they are. I put everyone into one of two columns. They're either an asset or they're a liability, period. There's nothing in between for me. If you are someone's "confused", they're a liability. If they are unintentionally hurting me, they're a liability. If they're not supporting me, they're a liability. They are not a "buddy who's gone bad". They're a liability for me and my group.

And even though it's not the only way to figure it out, social media is a great place to filter for whether the people in your life are assets or liabilities. A lot of these people who would go into the liabilities category right now are actually assets. They're just confused for a moment. Someone can go from being an asset to a liability and go back to being an asset. But if they keep going back and forth over and over the year, what's going to happen is the individual becomes a liability.

First thing you have to do if you want to collect assets in your life is quit buying liabilities and quit hanging out with liabilities. And in order to consistently do that, you have to understand that everything in your life is either an asset or it's a liability, whether it's intentionally or unintentionally.

When you don't look at whether things and people are assets and liabilities, the moment you're unwilling to confront your friends, your family, your employees, your co-workers — the moment you're not willing to accept that they're walking liabilities, when they are — that's the moment you've become a liability yourself.

YOUR 36 INCHES

The other category of intangible asset (or liability) is your skills. What are your skills? Are the skills you possess assets? How do they help you produce income or build the relationships that help you produce income?

Your goal, with the skills you develop, if you want to be able to put them into the asset column is simple. You have to figure out how to get the people around you focused on your agenda and your outcomes. You do that by focusing on the 36 inches around you. If you would just mind your own business, not let the people around you distract you into worrying about their 36 inches, you could achieve anything.

That's one of the biggest secrets to creating wealth and escaping the middle-class trap. You have to learn the skills required to get the people around you to worry about your 36 inches. When they're paying attention to what you're doing, they're not paying attention to what they're doing. Try to get them focused on your agenda, in a positive way. But even when they're focused on criticizing or accusing you, they can't be focused on their 36 inches, can they?

You can't hate and create at the same time. It's absolutely impossible. You can't criticize somebody else and take your own inventory at the same time. You can't correct someone else and correct you. You're doing one of the other. So, at 25 years old, I told myself, "Let me just handle my 36 inches."

"You can't hate and create at the same time!"

You have your hands full with your own thoughts and ideas. And then you add a few other people to your circle: your spouse, you kids, and it becomes even more complicated. Now add an employee. Add two employees. Add four employees. Add 10 employees. Add a bad employee. Add two bad employees. Add a good employee that goes bad.

That's what business is. It becomes very complicated. So, the most important thing is that you need to be in the best shape of your life. That's why I say, "40 hours of work / 7 hours of self-enhancement." 80 hours of work you might want to kick the enhancement time up.

Personal enhancement means: What are you reading, studying and learning? Who are you letting into your life? And most important, how do you execute? Your skills in the asset column are all about execution. How do you execute? And when you're all broken up, beat up and confused, how can you execute? And if you're distracted, it's impossible.

The word "execute" means to kill something. It means to finish something, to put into effect a plan, order or course of action, to carry out a death sentence. You have to be ready to carry out death sentences. Find something and go get it.

When my daughters were still kids, they couldn't set serious goals. They couldn't execute a plan or even do something as simple as fly on a commercial airplane yet. One of my daughters had never been on a commercial airline. She asked, "Dad, will I ever get to fly on a non-private jet?" I hope not!

One of the teachers at the school that my girls used to attend asked me, "Mr. Cardone, are you going to teach your daughters how to read?" And I said, "Nope. You teach them how to read. I'm going to teach them how to do stuff that matters most. And what I mean by that is, it's that teacher's job to teach them how to read and write. It's my job to teach them how to multiply! I taught my daughter how to count to ten and then multiply — skip to 100! You don't need to learn all those other numbers man, they're dumb numbers. Go to ten and multiply.

I focus on teaching them how to do stuff that matters most, like how to meet people and how to get what they want by getting up on their feet and walking up to somebody and introducing themselves and saying, "I can do anything and this is what I want from you."

So that's my job, to teach my kids the skills they actually need to create wealth and success. And that's also my job with you in the next three chapters. To teach you the skills required to escape the middle-class trap. The plan you're about to develop and execute will work to create wealth in any area: money, health, friends, fans, if you need investors for your ideas and it'll certainly work in real estate. Welcome to the Wealth Creation Formula. You're going to enjoy this.

SECTION 1
Score System

MONEY TRAPS
Score Range
15-61

If you scored between
15-30

Make a note of identifying which steps you already do and how to continue to repeat them so you can move to the next step of the formula.

If you scored between
31-45

Note the specific pieces of these traps you are falling in and find ways to optimize the way you go through these steps of the formula.

If you scored between
46-61

You should review this section carefully. These specific traps seem to be severely holding you back. Make sure you write down actionable items to break the cycle of these traps.

XI.
1st Phase: Earned Income

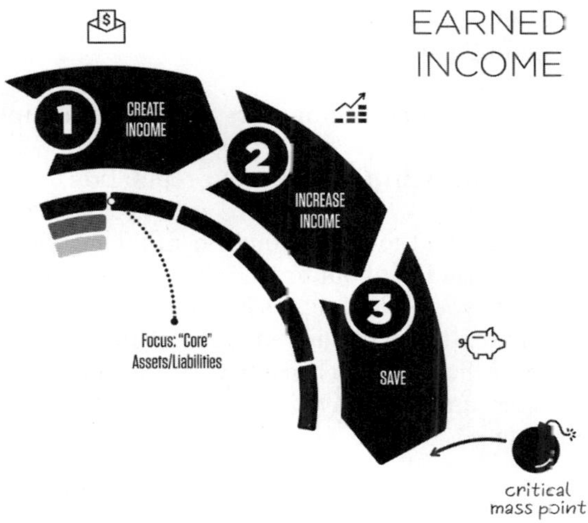

In this first phase of your Wealth Creation Formula, you're going to follow three steps. The goal of this phase is to stay focused on increasing your core income assets, while minimizing core liabilities. The goal is to max out your ability to generate "earned income". In this chapter, you're going to get clear on...

1. **Why you want to focus on creating income with your current job**

2. **The best ways to increase your income inside your job**

3. **How to save money to invest with** (not for a "rainy day")

Your core assets (or liabilities) in this phase are the ones you have at the start of this wealth creation formula...

YOUR CORE ASSETS:

Core cash flow assets: your job (paycheck)

Core belief assets: your work ethic, your beliefs about your potential and possibilities

Core skill assets: selling, persuasion, self-discipline

Core relationship assets: your reputation

At the top of the list though, is your job and the income it produces. Because I'm about to show you the reason that, despite what anyone tells you, it's impossible to get rich without income. It cannot happen. You haven't known a single person in your lifetime who became wealthy, not even from an inheritance, and who stayed wealthy without continuing to create income.

STEP #1: CREATE INCOME

At this stage, in Step #1 of your Wealth Creation Formula, "income" is basically the money you earn from a job. Later income is also the money that comes from a stock, i.e., dividend income. Here in your first pass of Step #1 though, you're going to focus on earning income from your job.

And sure, there are some things about earned income that make it less attractive than other ways to create wealth. A lot of people say earned income is the least desired, because it's the most heavily taxed. But you're never going to get away with not paying taxes.

The best way to think about it is, you should want to create more income to be taxed on, until one day you don't have what can technically be defined as "income" anymore.
Look, everyone knows the whole game is rigged. But if you understand the entire Wealth Creation Formula, you can get the stacked deck to work for you. You just need to know how this rigged game is played. But no matter what way you cut it, the starting place is income.

So, there's one question you need to ask yourself, without delay, "What can I do today, right now, that will create income? Let's say you don't have a job. We all started without jobs. What can you do without a job to create income today? That's first.

And second, what is the target for your income? As an example, let's say that my daughter, Sabrina, wants to create income. Do you think the very first thing I would have done is send her to college? Absolutely not. Why would I have waited when there were things she could have been doing when she was younger to create income.

But what happens in our system today is people say, "Hey, I wanna get a job. Let me go to college." That's ridiculous. You don't need to go to college to get a job and get income. You don't actually even need to learn a skill in order to get income, to grow income, to grow many streams of income, to start from poverty and get somewhere.

All you need is this plan — your clear strategy with a well laid out process. The better you understand each of the steps: create, increase, save, invest, the better you will do. And notice that nowhere in there does it say, "Go to college." Naturally, you will have to learn something. You'll have to learn how to create revenue and get better at creating revenue. And once you learn to create revenue, you're going to want to learn how to get more effective at it. That way you can create more revenue in shorter periods of time.

Depending on what you're earning right now, which of the following six income avatars are you?

1. **Petey Po'Boy** - you currently have very little or no income to speak of, digging in your parents' couch for change.

2. **Gary Gov'ment** - you get paid on the first Monday of every month and all your money, or at least most of it, comes from the government.

3. **Sandi Singlemom** - making $19K a year with a family of one or two, or a single mother only making $19K.

4. **Mikey Middleman** - right smack dab in the middle-class trap, as that at $50K per year mark, with just enough money left over to go to the movies once a month and buy some new tennis shoes, if they're on sale.

5. **Cathy Comfybutt** - you've been making somewhere between $50K and $100K for years, and you have more money than most of the people in your neighborhood; better car; never worrying about your car payment or your house payment. Your kids have the things they need, but you never have enough to make a big play, but you want to get into a whole new range.

6. **Barry Bigspender** - with one income, making $400K, and you seem to be sitting pretty, but I know the truth...

I work with a lot of people who make $400K, $600K, $800K, even a million dollars yearly. But it's only one flow of income and my question to them is, "When are you going to make a decision to get wealthy?"

I was doing a conference for a large insurance group. The average earner in the room made $970K last year before taxes — $970K worth of income. Unless they've worked through all nine steps on the wealth wheel, they're in step one. And that, by the way, is the entry to wealth creation. It is the front door you must walk through, and always will need to in order to create wealth.

When I was 25 years old, I had less money than when I was eight. How is that even possible? When my daughters were younger, if I wanted to help them create wealth, instead of sending them to school, I would have given them this; focus on wealth and how you create it.

There are two points you want to take away. First, you need a target for your income. Wherever you're at right now, where do you want to be? You must have a target. People are operating without target income. And honestly, most people have no clue what they actually make. The only time they know what they make is when they negotiate their salary.

So, the first thing is to set a target. You've got to have a target. And the second thing ties into what I've been talking about in this book, your beliefs as either an asset or a liability. You have to know that anyone can create new income.

Anyone, you could be broke right now. You could be on a desert island, with an Internet connection and create income. It doesn't matter. This is your entry. This is your front door. And you must fortify this income and make it strong. You have to add value to what you do to make it bigger. And you want to make sure, even if you currently feel like you hate your job or hate your current position in life, that you never complain.

Never ever complain about your front door income. Never, no matter how small it is, no matter how dirty you have to get your hands. I've done jobs that I felt like I hated. I still do jobs today that I feel like I hate. But I never ever complain about that income. The same person that complains about their core earned income will spend time, energy, and even money to work at something else.

So never complain about the income you make. Never complain about that job. Your job at that point is creating income. Then, you want to expand this income. Make sure you have a job that will be there for you tomorrow. Once you make sure you have that job, fortify that position, okay?

Be the go-to person. Eliminate any idea of competition around the world. Make sure no piece of technology can ever replace you. Make sure you're that person in that organization that everyone else will want to continue to send this income to. All wealth creation starts with this front door — with a decision and fortifying that one spot.

Make sure your position cannot be shipped overseas, replaced by another position or anything else. Understand this with wealth creation. Most people don't know how to make money. You need to have a position where people happily give you money for that position. This is your first step. Create income. We're going to build on this in the sections that follow.

STEP #2: INCREASE INCOME

Once you've established and opened your earned income front door and fortified it, you're ready to move to the second step. Your focus in this step is increasing the income you've established. You're going to ask yourself, "How do I take this income I've created from this first job without getting a second, third job or fourth job?" You're going to increase the income of the first stream that you created. And at some point, you've got to confront the boogieman in the room; the word nobody wants to do: SELLING.

See, once you have a job, fortify that job and continue to fortify it. Don't start a new business yet. Don't "save" yet. Don't invest yet. Your second move is to increase your current income, wherever it's coming from. Make it bigger in size, amount, intensity or degree. Make it juicier. You want to increase the size of it.

And don't think small either. Ask yourself, "What if I could 10X my income?" Think about it. How much would your life change? It would change a bunch, wouldn't it? First time I was asked that question it rocked my world! I was making $60K a year. I lived in Lake Charles, Louisiana. I was in debt, working my butt off every day.

When a man I knew asked me that question, my initial thought was, "That's impossible." Then I said to myself, "But what if?" That question sat with me and it still sits with me. "What if I could 10X my income?" Back then I didn't know how to do it. The business I was in, there was nobody in that space that was doing that kind of income. It haunted me though. What if I really could 10X my income? What would I have to do? Who would I need to meet? What would I need to learn?

Just to be completely transparent, the first 12 months after that question was asked of me, I did not 10X my income. But I did jump up to $350K, so I seven x-ed it. And all of a sudden, I got all this enthusiasm.

Now, over the years, I've continued to ask myself that question, because I know it starts with the mind. I think you'd agree with that if you think small, you get small. But once you have the right mindset, the right strategy, the right vehicle and the right people, it really is possible. So, once you get your head right, you've got to ask yourself if you're in the right vehicle and if so, do you have the right people around you, then, what's the best strategy?

So, let's lay out a strategy for you. And even though you could be at one of a few different levels, I'll use the example of a strategy for someone in a standard job, trying to jump their salary up. As the head of multiple companies, I have no problem rewarding people who are producing income. As long as you're contributing to the company and can work out a better deal for yourself, you should do it. I've got sales guys making over half a million dollars a year. That's more than most doctors and lawyers make. And some of these guys have no formal education at all.

But it's not only the salespeople. Employees from across all my companies have added zeros to their paychecks. Another great example is my receptionist. She was able to make an extra six figures in commissions over and above her salary. Today, she holds a management position in my company — and makes even more. These people all have one thing in common: they're committed to creating more income and furthering their careers. And you should be too.

So, let's talk about your options of approach for this strategy. The question is really, should you go after a raise or a promotion? A lot of people want to increase their salary with a simple raise. But they don't consider the massive value that comes with a promotion instead of a raise.

Just asking for more money won't guarantee you success in the long run. Sure, you might get a raise today, but you're going to limit your future opportunities. Plus, why get a 3% raise when you could get a 30% increase through a promotion instead?

If you know how to sell yourself as an asset to the organization, then everyone wins. You put yourself in the spotlight for financial, professional, and personal growth. At the same time, you develop along with the company, over the years. So, I advise you to always aim for a promotion instead of a raise.

As an example, Jarrod Glandt is the President of Grant Cardone Enterprises. But he started from the bottom. Jarrod came across one of my videos online and called up my team. He asked for a chance to work with me. Eventually, he did.

He started at $2,500 per month, plus a small commission on deals he wrote.

He was putting in 150 to 200 calls a day, and he still wasn't where he wanted to be financially. It all changed when he used some of the techniques I'm sharing with you here to get his mindset and more importantly, his actions right.

Fast-forward to today and he's earning $2.5 million a year as an "intrapreneur" employee inside my company. He's my right-hand man, and he is the ultimate example of how maturing with a company can massively increase your income.

So, like I keep talking about, everything starts with your mindset and the actions it leads you to take. The things you say and do, your actions, are always going to follow what you think and what you believe. So, let's talk a little bit about the things you need to make sure you are thinking right about.

Here are some things you should never let yourself believe or say inside your head. If you do, they will leak out as counterproductive statements when you're talking to the people around you, including whoever the decision-maker is in charge of raises and promotions.

Things to Avoid Thinking, Believing or Saying:

- "I've been here X many years, so I deserve way more money."
- "I work way harder than everyone else around me, so I deserve acknowledgment and a promotion."
- "This other person makes X amount of money more..."
- "If I don't get X more, I'll have to look for work elsewhere."

Instead of thinking any of those things, and rather than just asking for more money, ask how you can bring more value to the company. Ask things like:

> **"What's your opinion of my work so far?"** That gives you an idea what position you're in. It will help you negotiate to increase your income. Or ask,
>
> **"What can I do for the company that you could pay me X amount more for?"** Do this to offer value and solutions. Or, best of all, become a deal maker and ask,
>
> **"If I can reach this target, would you agree to increase my salary by X?"** In that case, you're assuming responsibility and taking pressure off your employer.

Remember that leaders love performance-based compensation. It's rarely risky to propose something you can do that might add to the company's bottom line without a flat payout request. But one thing to make sure of is that you're not creating any kind of problem for your employer. So, know the specific amount you want. Having a clear target in mind will help you increase your odds of getting what you're looking for.

Next, get the timing right and don't catch them off guard. Set a time and place where you have the decision-maker's full attention. Then, prepare all the relevant information for a successful meeting. Remember the rule of "Show, don't tell." Make sure to demonstrate the value you've brought to the company up until now.

Have you boosted sales? Did you lead large-scale projects? Pull any numbers you have and include them in your proposal. Include things like: production statistics; successful projects; completed initiatives; and any team accomplishments — especially if you led them.

And make sure you share any proof you have related to whatever you present. So, on top of any numbers, bring the heat with some social proof. Things like: client testimonials; past performance reviews; and documented appreciation from co-workers.

Then, finally, paint a picture of the future. How will you and the company grow from now on, especially with you in your new role? Create an outline of projected growth based on the data you have. After that, lay out the plan with all the action steps you'll take to get there.

Another thing you can do is practice your proposal. Every morning, my sales guys start the day by doing one-on-one role-playing. They practice every possible scenario they could face with a client. It gives them the space to fail, make mistakes, and learn from them — without losing sales. I advise you to treat your job salary increase proposal the same way.

Before the big day comes around, rehearse everything you want to put on the table. You can role-play with anyone. Grab a close friend or family member and walk through any reaction your boss might have. When money is on the line, you don't want to leave anything to chance.

At the end of the day, regardless of promotions or whatnot, there's one thing that has always won the day for me — sales. When I fully committed to selling, the whole game changed and I started making REAL money.

Remember, everyone is a salesperson, no matter what their job title is. Get sold on that fact, and you'll get what you want. I was telling you earlier that all my employees have the opportunity to sell and make commissions.

Even if your organization doesn't currently offer this, why not be the one to pitch it? For you, it's the only guaranteed way to control — and 10X — your income. For your employer, it's another person directly involved in increasing the company's revenue.

However you approach it, you need to get better at increasing income. You need to get better during Step #2 at what you're doing. Get better at your current situation. Add revenue to your current company. Don't get another job. Sales is the way to control income, to connect to revenue in your company, it is the best way to create an increase in income, without losing focus.

And ultimately, remember that this isn't only about money, it's about thinking like a wealthy person in every category of life. Think in abundance, prosperity and wealth. Don't worry about losing in one small area, because you're always increasing in income overall – in other words, the things coming "in" to you.

And a big key to this is to account for whatever your income is. Most people don't even know what their income is. They know they make $40K or $45,000 a year. But really, how much do you make? Ask yourself. Do you know the exact number to the penny? Because if you don't know the exact number to the penny, you're not truly grateful for what you have. And if you're not grateful and you don't acknowledge and you don't pay attention, it's going to go away.

How much do you actually make? How much do you actually keep? Are you willing to confront it? Most people never want to really look at the situation. Then they come up with reasons why they never created wealth the rest of their life. But when the people who create wealth look at it, they ask themselves, "How do I create income? How do I increase it? How do I save it? How do I invest it? How do I create multiple flows? How do I increase those flows to make them bigger and bigger and bigger?"

So how much do you actually make now and how much do you really keep? I'm going to bring you through the whole formula. In step #3, we'll get to the bottom of how much you should set aside. First, we create the income, then we increase the income. Then we set it aside – ALL of it.

STEP #3: SAVE (40/40/20)

This step is called "save", but don't get confused. This is not "saving for a rainy day." I call this "Set it ALL aside." This is the difference in what you used to earn and what you earn now. You went from $45K to $60K, or $80K to $120K, or $120K to $200K. I want you to set that difference aside — all of it... every penny!

Welcome to the 40/40/20 Rule. If you stick to this one rule, that most people just completely don't get, it will unlock the entire wealth creation process for you.

Let's start with the fact that 40% of your income already gets set aside. So, you are capable of doing this. What I mean is, 40% of your income goes to the IRS. And you probably hate the IRS as much as me and everyone else, right? But you're paying them 40%, aren't you? So, if you'll pay the IRS, someone we all hate, 40%, can you agree that you deserve to at least pay yourself 40%?

What I mean is, you've figured out how to pay 40% to the IRS — people who don't trust you with your own money. That's why they take their cut before you get paid. The law says that your employer has to withhold the tax man's cut from you. And honestly, that is a good financial decision. You've got to render unto Caesar that which is Caesar's, like Jesus said.

So just do the same for yourself. Put 40% aside, as if it doesn't exist, just like the IRS makes you do. Then, live on the remaining 20%. This is where it becomes difficult. You must seriously live only on the 20%, without changing your standard of living until the 20% changes. Never cheat on your money the way my buddy Cody did when he pulled up to my place in a rented Lamborghini a while back.

I love the guy, but that was stupid. I asked him, "Cody, what are you doing man?" "It's no big deal, Grant. It's just $1,700." But, to me it is a big deal, because you know what it says to me? It says he's not disciplined with his money. It's like knowing a friend is cheating on their spouse. You can still love them, but it makes you think differently about them, right? You have to be disciplined with your money. It's as simple as that.

You and your money have a relationship. And just like any relationship, believe me when I tell you, if you cheat on your money, your money will cheat on you. If you ignore your money, your money will ignore you. If you don't take care of your money, your money won't take care of you. As much as some folks might not like wealthy people — their kids may have a drug problem; their marriage may be falling — but wealthy people accumulate a lot of money because they pay attention to it.

They may not have figured out their marriage or their kids, but that's got nothing to do with money. They just didn't take the time to figure out the other relationships, I did not change my standard of living until my 20% changed. I've always paid myself that 40%, just like I've always paid the IRS theirs. I've been audited four times and I think they got $1,500 from me on one of the audits. And you know they have to find something, even when there's really nothing there.

The 20% is what I still live on. It's how I make all of my decisions in my personal life and in my business. First, 40% goes to the tax man. Next, 40% gets set aside, ultimately for investments. In my business it goes to feed the "beast", the advertising and the marketing. Then, 20% is what I live on.

And what happens if you can't live on that 20%? What do you have to do? You either lower your standard of living, control your standard of living, or you increase your overall 100%. It's as simple as that. That way you're not out buying Richard Mille watches and Gucci shoes, because you can't!

Don't play yourself. You're not fooling anyone else with your Richard Mille watch and your Gucci shoes. Those things are not going to get you a meeting with anyone who actually matters. It's what you have to say about your product or your service. How does it solve someone's problem? That's all anyone really cares about at the end of the day.

NUTSHELL TIME

So, in a nutshell, the first 40% comes right off the top for the tax man. Then 40% gets set aside. And you have to live within the remaining 20%, until you hit critical mass with what you've set aside. People always ask what that "critical mass" amount is. I never answer directly because it depends on the goals you set. Those are personal to you. But let's say it's somewhere between $50K and $250K.

In the next step, you're going to begin investing, but you want to make sure you don't invest too early with that 40% you set aside. Wait for it to hit whatever you decide is your critical mass amount. In the meantime, you should be focusing on building up your skills, specifically your sales skills. Your goal should be getting into a position where you can control and increase your income, ideally through some kind of commission-based position.

And this amount that you save, setting it all aside all ties in with the "Job Hate" trap and it's the answer to both the "Piggy

Bank" trap and "Golden Years" trap. But you may be thinking, "Hey Grant, wait a minute. It sounds like you're telling me to save. I thought you told me not to save?".

Nope. I said to "set it aside", instead of saving. In other words, don't make the mistake of trying to save your way to some kind of "rainy day" or for your "golden years". You absolutely, positively need to continually increase your little "money baby" stash that you set aside. The key is "out of sight, out of mind". Because, while you're increasing your income and maxing it out, you want to keep your "money baby" stash off to the side and not even need to think about it.

But you've got to have the discipline to live within your means, within that 20%. Focus almost all your time and energy on developing your core assets, mainly your skills and your beliefs and max out the income potential. Then, once you hit critical mass with your 40% set aside, you're going to start the next step, Step #4 up. That means figuring out where to point your 40% set aside so it starts producing "money babies".

It can be real estate or buying an existing business, really anything that produces more cash flow, with the minimum amount of time and effort required on your part — think passive. It also includes investing in you by educating yourself in a way that builds up the skills that produce and maintain your cash flow.

If you're inside someone else's business, look for ways to create a bigger impact within the business in a way that allows you to create extra income, without costing your employer anything.

Do this rather than trying to create a "side hustle" and splitting your focus (which is the approach a lot of people take), try to find a second flow of income inside your current employer's business.

It's all "found" money. First flow and max it out, then, once you hit critical mass, figure out how to deploy your 40% set aside stash so it starts producing money for you with the minimum amount of effort and time required by you.

But here's the catch... There's always one of those, right? In order to do all that, the first thing you've got to do is figure out what you need to change in your life and what you have to give up. As an example, in the first three sections of this book, you should have given up believing the myths and pretenses you had about the middle class. That's one big thing you can and should have given up at this point. But what else do you have to give up? Are there any relationships, assets or any habits that will interfere with your escape from roadkill, to rich, to wealthy?

But you need to understand the whole process. This is what happens to people. It's why people lose their wealth mindset — why they never get to millions. They interrupt the process, so your goal, at this point right here, is to save 40% of everything that comes in. No watches, no new clothes, no new cars. Save it all, so that one day you'll actually have something to invest.

Your step here is not to invest money. Do not send the money to a 401(k). Don't buy any real estate or stocks at this point. All you want to do right now is set your money aside. And by the way, it's your money for the very first time.

◆◆

SECTION 2
Score System

EDUCATION TRAPS
Score Range
5-39

If you scored between
5-17

Make a note of identifying which steps you already do and how to continue to repeat them so you can move to the next step of the formula.

If you scored between
18-29

Note the specific pieces of these traps you are falling in and find ways to optimize the way you go through these steps of the formula.

If you scored between
30-39

You should review this section carefully. These specific traps seem to be severely holding you back. Make sure you write down actionable items to break the cycle of these traps.

XII.
2nd Phase: Investment Income

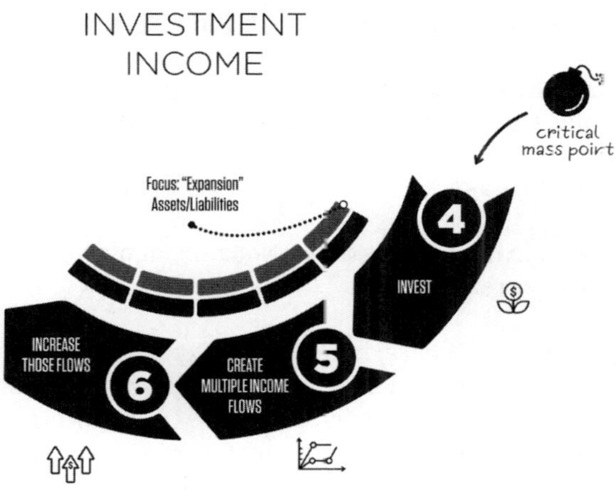

In this second phase of your Wealth Creation Formula, you're going to do the next three steps — steps 4-6. In this phase the goal is to expand by investing, only once you hit a critical mass point with your savings. After that you're going to create multiple flows of income, then increase those. In this chapter, you're going to get clear on...

1. **Why you want to set a specific "critical mass" number for your savings, before you ever invest!**

2. **How to create multiple income flows without becoming schizophrenic**

3. **The exact right way to increase your income flows and never back slide toward the left-behind class again!**

Your "expansion" assets (or liabilities) in this phase are the ones you build after you out a foundation of income and savings in place.

YOUR EXPANSION ASSETS:

Core cash flow assets: expansion investment income

Core belief assets: confidence as you shift from this second phase to the third phase — "Wealth Scaling"

Core skill assets: marketing, networking, investing

Core relationship assets: your social network, influencer relationships

At the top of the list here, in terms of "Expansion" assets is your network and confidence. Another key consideration is knowing exactly what your "critical mass" number is and waiting to hit that number before investing.

STEP #4: INVEST

Step #4 is the step that most people prematurely move to, because they've been told to get there early. But that's bad advice. You don't want to start investing early. You don't want to start with a "little". And you definitely need to know what you're doing when you're investing.

Always stay aware of which step you're on in the Wealth Creation Formula. It's all part of a process that never stops. In Step #1 you've gone out and created income. It could have been \$10. It could have been \$10,000. It could have been \$10 million. In Step #2 you've increased that income. Maybe you've doubled it or tripled it. Hopefully you've been able to 10X it! Then, in Step #3 you've set it aside — ALL OF IT! That's every penny the tax man doesn't take and every penny you don't absolutely need to live on.

You have to understand the wealth wheel is an ongoing process. Its momentum is going to continue as you create wealth. It does not stop moving or pause or freeze in time like it looks here as an infographic. You create income. You increase income. You save income, you set it aside. And the only reason to save money, to set it aside, is what your mommy and daddy didn't tell you. The real reason to set it aside is not for a rainy day or for your golden years. It's to take that money and multiply by investing it.

"Investing" means spending money with the expectation of achieving a profit. As an example, let's use Starbucks Coffee. That company takes cups of coffee that cost them 10 or 15 cents and sells them for $4 to coffee junkies like me! But in order to do that they had to invest in machines, in real estate, in marketing, in employees, because Uncle Grant likes his four shots in a giant cup, filled up 2/3 of the way, with the rest filled with foam.

They paid people to harvest the coffee beans; they ground it down and put it in shops and stores all over the world. They made it available 24/7. So, the only reason to have money is to: one, buy essentials; and two, invest in ways that create "money babies"...

Money was originally invented so people could trade things easily, without having to exchange a goat for a chicken. It just became a little difficult if you wanted to do that at scale. Someone said, "Hey, why don't we create some money? We'll place some value on that money so Joe can trade money with John for the chicken, so Jim can go to Mike, the goat guy, and buy the goat and so on.

Now that we have money, a couple thousand years later, how do I take that money and create wealth with it? The answer is simple. You do it by investing. You'll never get wealthy if you don't invest. You have to do both things. Earn and invest in order to create wealth. I know people who earn a lot of money. For instance, NBA players earn a lot of money — unbelievable amounts of money in many cases. And rich kids with parents who put $80K per month into their trust fund have it too. And yet, in many cases they have nothing to show because they never learned how to invest it.

Again, investing means spending money with the expectation of profit, not spending money just for the sake of it. So, no matter where you're at on the wealth wheel. You may be at a different level of investing though, with a different thinking. Because if you're a rich kid with a trust fund, you still need to learn how to go out and create income, how to increase it, how to set it aside and how to invest it.

Even if someone was born into a rich family, it doesn't mean they're wealthy. They may have money, so you could call them rich, but nobody knows them. People don't like them. Nobody trusts them. Their success is determined by their courage, their creativity and their ability to actually make the world a better place. That $80K they get every month doesn't change anything. That's not wealth. It's only money. Anyone can be rich. Not just anyone can be wealthy. Being wealthy takes discipline, determination and you have to know what it means to really invest: to devote one's time, effort, or energy to a particular undertaking with the expectation of a desired outcome.

When I post something on Facebook that is investing. When I travel to Toronto to speak to a large group, and I pay for the flight, it takes my time and mental focus. That is an investment. The question is, what investments and at what level? What do you start with when you're broke?

Well, let me answer that in a way that might not make sense when you first read it. When I was first starting out at 25 years old, I didn't invest in anything outside myself. For eight years, between the ages of 25 and 33, every investment I made went right into things that were three feet around me. If it wasn't around me, close to me, next to me, I didn't invest in it.

By the way, whether we realize it or not, every one of us is investing every day, in time, and focus and energy, at the very least. But when it comes to investing money, most people invest too little, not too much, and too early, not too late. People get taught, just start little, start early. It'll turn into something. That's not true though.

"INVESTMENT" CRITICAL MASS

In nuclear physics, "critical mass" is when you have the minimum amount of a material needed to create a self-sustaining fission reaction. So, it's the amount of fuel you need for something to happen and to keep happening.

This concept is similar to the way I think about investment energy. The exact "money" critical mass depends on your own personal situation. But you definitely want to KNOW your number before moving into the second phase of the Wealth Creation Cycle.

For most people, you want to wait until you've set aside somewhere between $100K and $250K before you ever, ever, ever make an investment outside of you, YOURSELF. This range is totally made up and arbitrary by the way, but I've got to pick something tangible. People ask me every day, "Hey, man, I got $20K. Should I start investing now?" No. Not unless it's something inside your 36-inch circle. You don't have enough. "I got 40 grand." You don't have enough yet. "I got 60 grand." Dude, don't just go collect another $40K.

And let me make this totally clear for you. It's not like $60K isn't enough to actually invest and turn a meaningful profit. That's not the point. I had to pick some number that shows that you've created enough money-discipline.

So, set a number between $100K and $250K as your "critical mass". Hitting whatever you set shows that you can do more than just earn income and increase it. It demonstrates that, in the process of earning and increasing, then setting money aside, you didn't create emergencies in your life that destroyed it. You've developed your money-discipline.

The thinking behind this is pretty simple. We all know people who reach certain levels of success, but continually sabotage themselves along the way. When you're able to hit critical mass like this, you've been developing your money-discipline, without creating a bunch of sabotaging acts along the way that destroy the money.

That's what so many people do at this point in the process. I picked a range. It could be right at $100K. It could be at $175K. Maybe it's not until you hit $250K. There's no scientific way of knowing. In my case, I told myself, "I'm gonna pick a number. So, I chose $100K and committed to it until I hit it — zero investments.

What you need to do between now and then is study. The only investments you're going to make are inside your 36-inch circle, things within your reach. If you need a secretary, if you need a receptionist, if you need a marketing plan, if you need to buy a car to get you back and forth to build your business, do it. No problem.

If you're a landscaper and you need to buy a lawn mower, that's an investment. Those are the "36-inch circle" investments I'm talking about early on, things that are close to you. Until you hit your critical mass, don't look to make other investments.

Before I made my first investment. I had a million dollars in a bank account and I took a third of it and threw it into a deal. But you better have some courage when you do that. People always say, "It takes money to make money." That's not true. It takes courage to make money. And the best way to develop courage regarding money is to create more money.

In my case, I took a third of my money and pushed it to a deal. So, when people say, "Man, you're brave about investing money." I'm thinking to myself, "Dude, I got twice that sitting in a bank. I'm not going to put that at risk." And here's what you can do to reduce risk on investment you do make. When you make that first big investment, with that $100K or $150K or a quarter million dollars, look for deals that are as "ironclad" as you can find, OK?

Is there any such thing as a deal that's guaranteed to pay you? Nothing's guaranteed, but some things are "ironclad". Think of it the same way a jury thinks of "beyond a reasonable doubt" when they're deciding whether someone has committed a crime. There's no way of knowing for sure if someone is guilty of a crime. When the prosecutor makes a case that's ironclad, covers all the bases and presents evidence that's irrefutable, the jury can see it.

The first thing to think about is forecastable return. Look for at least a 6-12% return on any investment you're thinking about getting into. The first investment I ever made was my apartment deal for $350,000. That deal appreciated over time, provided me with cash flow, and is now the reason why I'm able to raise millions of dollars in investment capital. I'm able to invest my money in huge deals that the average person would never have access to. I earned, then set aside, then I earned again and set aside more. I kept doing that until I could use that money to purchase an investment, not put that money into any middle-class trap.

That original deal provided me with monthly income and a nice annual rate of return. You don't need to go for a 50% or

100% return on investment. Those types of deals are not built for the long term. It's really speculation. I want you to get rich for sure. If you look for 6-12% returns, you'll be on your way.

Warren Buffett says that there are two rules when it comes to successful investing:

RULE #1: Never lose money.

RULE #2: Don't forget Rule No. 1.

That's the way to think about a deal being "ironclad". Look for deals that are so ironclad that the world would have to be hit by an Independence Day meteor to not pay you. For an ironclad deal to go upside down, the whole world would have to blow up. Evaluate based on downside. In other words, think through every worst-case scenario; the economy goes bad, jobs stop, there's a terrorist attack in the neighborhood, whatever. Everything, everything changes, everything gets ugly. Do I still want to be in this deal? If the answer is yes, buy the deal.

And really, the best way to think about things is based on what stage you're in. So, in the earliest stages, you should only be investing in you. This is where you're buying educational programs. You're going to conferences and you're investing in trips to get around people. That's why you need lots of money. You need to meet great people.

The one other consideration centers around the standout asset (or liability), your reputation, the network it helps you build and the gravity it can create. Because, the thing is, expanding and refining your reputation and your network are actually key to getting the most out of your other assets.

I like to say that "if people don't know you, they won't follow you." That means that the cash flow you need in order to make this will never fully develop if you're veiled in obscurity. In other words, you can't get cash and you can't get deals, if you're not on the radar.

Most of the middle class lives in obscurity by default. No one knows them. Getting known, at least in your circles, is a key part of the Wealth Creation Formula. Getting known = money grown. Whether you know it or not, 90% of your problems stem from obscurity. So many of your biggest problems will suddenly disappear once you learn the secrets of reputation creation.

So, in the first stages, you don't need to go on a vacation, but if you're going to go on a vacation, go on a vacation where you can meet somebody. That basically is an investment, not a memory, right? If you don't have the money and your trip is about staying at a Holiday Inn where breakfast is for free, you don't have the money to make that trip yet.

Always ask yourself, "Who can I meet for dinner?" or "Who can I bring?" Those are investments. Now, if you go to dinner with your spouse, and it's just the two of you having a good time, that's one thing. If you go to your dinner with your spouse and you can meet two clients, that's another thing. That's an investment. I'd rather see you spend more money and make an investment that expands you.

The idea is to prepare you for the next step on the wealth wheel, multiple flows of income. Your clients, your friends, your exposure and your brand are a big part of that, right? We want to get you more flows. More flows create more confidence, more courage and more wealth.

STEP #5: CREATE MULTIPLE FLOWS OF INCOME

Never depend on one income flow. Today, I probably have 50 or 60 flows of income. I quit counting. I'm like, "Okay, that's a lot of flows, man!" I have so many, I had to give them all names, instead of numbers. You want to think in terms of symbiotic, close and connected.

When I started as a salesperson, I needed a job. I was in the unemployment line. My uncle asked me, "What are you doing?" I said, "I'm trying to get income." He's like, "Your job is to go get a job, a real job, not a check from the government."

He took me down and introduced me to a guy. The guy hired me and gave me a draw every month. I think it was $250 every two weeks to work there and talk to customers. That's called a draw in that business.

He gave me a draw or an "advance". That was income. Okay? I was 25 years old, I had no money. I had no credit. I had no personal self-worth. I didn't even like myself. I'm telling people, don't even spend time with me, dude. My mom's telling people, "Keep your kids away from my kid." I was a wreck. I had one tiny little source of income. So, the first thing I had to do was ask myself, "How do I increase my income from $250 to $500?"

The answer was simple: learn how to actually get the company's products successfully into the hands of someone who will pay for them. That was my first introduction to how economies work. If you want revenue, you get revenue. A lot of people just stop with the draw, they just stop with their salary. Look for the commission connected to the company that you work at. Ask yourself, "Hey, what can I add to that?"

For me, I had a draw, then I had commissions. All of a sudden, my income went from $520 a week to$2,500 a week because I learned how to get the commission. It exploded five times. I was 25 years old. I committed to getting my money right, my life. He gave me a draw and I wrapped it with a commission.

I learned early on that my ability to create a multiple flow was all connected to bringing leads to the service department and the repair department.

They sold warranties in this company and they paid other companies outside that company for leads to sell these warranties. Since they were already paying other companies for leads to service and repairs, I wondered whether I could get paid the same amount for a lead. The answer was, "Hell yes!"

And the next thing you know, what do I have? Multiple income flows! I made buddies with people that I competed with. I couldn't sell every customer, but if I referred someone to their product, they would pay me for the referral!

I started buying our product and when the place I was at didn't want to do a deal, I would buy it and sell it from home. So, at 26 years old, I had these sources of income. I had my draw, I had my commission, I had leads to service, I had finance.

So, there I was working in one place, the same place, the same period of time, about like 12 hours a day, and I had seven streams of income from all these other sources. I didn't move locations. I stayed in the same spot. I didn't go get a second, third or fourth job.

The secret key is that you have to master one environment before you start trying to control environments. So, when you create multiple flows of income, you don't leave that job. Start with flows that are symbiotic, connected, complimentary — flows that are close to you.

Let's say you're a college student and you're working part-time at Starbucks. What can you do that would not cause you to miss your studies, while adding money? Look around your environment. There's something you can do. Trust me.

I was at Starbucks this morning in an extremely affluent area called Bal Harbour. The thing I noticed was that the tip jar was turned around, facing the barista. The sign on the tip jar read, "Hey, we appreciate tips.", but I couldn't even see it. It was 7:30am and that Starbucks opens at 5:30. So, it was two hours in an extremely prosperous and affluent place.

There's only $1 in the tip jar. Why? Because it wasn't out in front. Nobody was taking the job of asking, seriously. A tip jar is the second flow, but you have to ask. You have to make it obvious. And as part of your main job, you have to add value. Make that second income flow as friction-free as possible.

It's key to remember that you're not looking for another job in the beginning. Look for two flows in the beginning that are connected before you move to disconnected flows and don't change locations. You don't want to learn a whole bunch of new stuff. What you want to do is stay in your location and figure out how to create a second, third or fourth flow. Ask yourself, "What can I do right now? What's available around me right now that's close and within arm's reach?" That will create a second flow.

Multiple streams of income are the key to making money without needing to focus on them — "while you sleep", as they say. However, so many people run this play the wrong way. To paint a picture for you, I am going to start with an example I heard of doing this "Create Multiple Streams of Income" step the wrong way.

Recently, an employee of mine told me that his landlord started making food deliveries to earn some extra cash. To say I was shocked would be an understatement. Don't get me wrong. There's nothing shameful about delivering food. What blew my mind was how dissimilar one stream of income was from his main venture — they didn't support one another.

Let me clearly define how you should look at cashing in from different sources. When you're making a decision about adding another income flow, consider something in the same industry or a parallel one. This approach allows these multiple flows to feed and fuel one another, which ensures their strength.

Now, let's say my employee's landlord owned a restaurant, then got all the fees and tips from delivering the food. That would be a different story. You're the one who knows the ins and outs of your industry better than anyone else. You know the problems you face on a daily basis. That's why one of the best ways to create an additional income flow is to invent a business solution that solves a problem in the space you're already in.

The possibilities are endless, and it's the way to make this technique work without running in circles. At the end of the day, multiple streams of income have to be tackled with a plan in mind. You have to be strategic about it. Otherwise, you're adding more shackles instead of working towards freedom.

And at this point on the wheel, when you start moving into creating multiple flows, there's one key expansion asset to focus on — your network. How can you meet people? How can you talk to people? How can you get to know them? How can you build rapport? How do you find out what their problems are? And, ultimately, how do you close them? When is it the right move?

These questions are all important, because as we approach the third phase on the Wealth Wheel, it's time to start looking for investors and opportunities. So, how do you build trust and how do you get people to know you, like you and want to do business with you? How do you get people to pay attention to you?

Remember, real wealth means creating multiple flows of valuable things, not just money. Friends, connections, fans support, brand awareness. Wealth is about everything. When you hear the word "wealth", think "wealth" and "abundance" in everything.

Remember that it's people who have the money, not machines, that will help you create wealth. Machines don't have your money. Even if it's encrypted currency, somebody owns that encrypted currency. Think about how you can connect with people. Currency is about your ability to communicate, get attention, build rapport, build trust, stay connected, and by doing that, you will create multiple flows of income.

STEP #6: INCREASE THOSE FLOWS

6

INCREASE THOSE FLOWS

Before I move into how to increase your multiple flows of income, I want to clearly define three words. The word "create", the word "multiple" and the word "flows" from the previous step on the wheel. It's important because you have to really understand the difference between "creating" flows and "increasing" them.

The word create is an unbelievably powerful word. It means to bring something into existence. It is literally a spiritual word. When you create something, it means you're making something out of nothing. The original word meant to produce. To create means to produce, and to do that you have to use something divine, like your intelligence or your creativity.

The point of this is, you're never truly "broke", not broke as long as you have creativity and the courage to create.

The word "multiple" means numerous, several, many. It comes from the Latin word multiplex: "involving many parts or relations; consisting of more than one complete individual".

And then the word "flows" means a steady continuous stream. So, it's something you can depend on. The word it derives from is "flood". Imagine being flooded with streams of income that are continuous.

Remember income and wealth don't need to be limited to money. Depending on where you're at on the wheel, it can be connections or fans or notoriety. Any of these things can live under the umbrella of valuable possessions, so they can be considered wealth, right? And, ultimately, what you're doing on the wealth wheel, as part of your wealth creation plan, is creating income, increasing income, saving it, investing it and creating multiple flows as part of your wealth-building process.

But when it comes to specifically increasing those flows, how do you do that? How do you take these two or three flows and increase them? You want to go wide, not just deep. The biggest key to increasing your flows is measuring. You have to measure things and never guess. If you have 5 or 10 multiple flows, know without a doubt, which 2-3 are the most likely to be increased with the least amount of effort, energy and most importantly, time from you.

Time is money, right? Where you put your time will equal whether or not you have money. Always pay close attention to your flows. Track them. Graph them. You need to be looking at graphs. What's going up? What's going down? What's staying flat? Anything that stays flat will fall. You need to measure these flows. That's the only way to acknowledge and validate them. You need to acknowledge them when they're good. Whenever you get a big push or a big pop — good job; great job; super job!

So, give freaking muscle to the muscle. Give support to the win. You need to celebrate when you're doing well. You need to give attention to each and every one of the moments when a flow wins for you. What you give attention to is what you're going to bring into existence.

And here's another time when you need to save, save, save! And this time I'm not talking only about money. I'm talking about time, energy and other resources. You don't have time for any BS. You want to get wealthy. Pay the price today so you can pay any, any price in the future.

◆◆◆

SECTION 3
Score System

ASSET TRAPS
Score Range
6-39

If you scored between
6-17

Make a note of identifying which steps you already do and how to continue to repeat them so you can move to the next step of the formula.

If you scored between
18-28

Note the specific pieces of these traps you are falling in and find ways to optimize the way you go through these steps of the formula.

If you scored between
29-39

You should review this section carefully. These specific traps seem to be severely holding you back. Make sure you write down actionable items to break the cycle of these traps.

XIII.
3rd Phase: Wealth Scaling

In this third and final phase of your Wealth Creation Formula, it's time for you to think about scaling the wealth you've created so far. The real problem most people have is they try to model what they see wealthy people do, but they just do it too soon. Timing is EVERYTHING! In this chapter, you're going to see...

1. **How to set your second critical mass point** (before making new kind of investments)

2. **What types of bigger investments to make at this level**

3. **How to finally diversify the RIGHT way!**

Your "scaling" assets (or liabilities) in this phase are the ones you want to develop now that you've managed to jump from merely being "rich" to becoming "wealthy"!

YOUR SCALING ASSETS:

Core cash flow assets: diversification investment income

Core belief assets: legacy and philanthropic mindset, where you begin to focus on the way you will be remembered

Core skill assets: marketing, networking, investing

Core relationship assets: team assets, high level alliances

At the top of the list here, in terms of "Scaling" assets is your brand, your legacy mindset and your team assets. Another key consideration is knowing exactly what your wealth scaling "critical mass" number is and waiting to hit that number before branching out into new types of investments.

STEP #7: SAVE (SOME MORE)

Step #7 is "Save." And you may be thinking to yourself, "Wait. I thought we already covered this step Uncle G." Nope. You have to learn how to save at this step on the wheel differently than you saved in step #3. Remember, during the first phase, you're creating income for the first time. Maybe you went from zero to $5K or $10K. I remember when I saved my first $8,000, I was like, "Oh my gosh, I have $8,000!"

Jean, the salesperson I worked with at the time, had also saved $8K. He went and blew his $8K and had to start over again from zero. I didn't. I invested it in myself — only myself.

Remember the 36-inch investment circle? Early on there's no money to invest. Once you create multiple flows and then increase those flows of income, you're going to find yourself "up".

Thanks to the Internet and other communication platforms, at no other time in the history of the planet has it been easier to create multiple flows of income, regardless of your age, your location or how much money you start with.

Let's say you've got some money set aside — maybe it's $100K $150K or $250K, whatever the number is, are you gonna be tempted now? The reason you create wealth is not so you can tell people, "I'm worth a billion dollars or a hundred million or $10 million." No one who truly understands what wealth really is walks around telling everyone that they're a millionaire. First of all, it's nothing to even brag about. You're still worried every second of every day about money. A million dollars is basically enough money to put you into anxiety.

At $10 million, you can relax a little. At $100 million, almost nothing matters. You can make some big plays. You're waiting for situations to happen so you can literally fly in and seize the opportunity. The point is, where you are on the wealth wheel puts you in a different frame of mind.

$180K does not put you into safety. That amount could be wiped out with one scare of cancer. You could be completely wiped out. I know people who've gone through $400K because their healthcare, that they thought would cover them, did not. You want to be safe with enough money so that you create enough lifeboats.

You need enough lifeboats in case one gets stuck, too many people get into one lifeboat or one side of the ship goes down. You want extra lifeboats to make sure you have an escape from danger. That's the purpose of saving money — to make sure your family and your future stay secure.

The rule of thumb at this point is not to make any new investments. You're not moving to this until you have at least a million dollars put away. Don't even consider it. How do you keep that money safe? That brings us to the idea of "sacred accounts". The first thing you need to do is set the intention that the accounts where you set aside your income during the Wealth Scaling phase are sacred. It could be checking, could be a money market. Money market basically is an account that you can't trade more than five times in a month.

You can't write a check out of it more than four or five times in a month. And it might pay you a little more than a checking account. Maybe it's in a savings account, where you have no restriction regarding how many times you can write checks. But you don't want to write checks out of this sacred account anyway.

You don't want to change anything that got you to where you are at this point. What happens is people put a quarter of a million away and start to think they need to buy an exotic car or a luxury watch. Don't do it. Don't buy ANYTHING yet, regardless of whether it's electric, gas, 8- or 12-cylinder! Did that get you to this point? No, it did not. Did a Rolex get you to that point? No.

What got you to where you are? If it did get you here, why change it? Just keep doing what you've been doing because it's working. Why does everybody feel like once they get a little bit of money in the bank, they have to demonstrate by celebrating with stupid purchases? You are still broke. Okay?

At this point, maybe you've got three, four or five flows of income coming in. That's great. You can be considered "rich", but you're not wealthy yet. The economy could suddenly shift. Entire industries have been taken down. So, your five flows could go to three flows tomorrow. Now, where are you at?

You could put that money in bonds. You could put it in the stock market. You could buy a mutual fund. The truth is, your money gets trapped when you do that, like we talked about in The "Overdiversification" Trap. So don't do any of those things right now. When you invest at the Wealth Scaling level, you have to be fearless. And part of that fearlessness, that courage, comes from being so sure about the investment that there really is little to actually fear. But still, there's no such thing as a 100% sure thing. And when you invest at this level you need a lot of money, and it doesn't take money to make money, the way they say. At this level, it takes courage to make money. I know people with money that don't have the courage to use it.

When I was in this phase on the Wealth Wheel, I had over a million dollars sitting in an account. Could I have put some of it at risk as a Wealth Scaling investment? Sure, but did I? No!

I had over a million dollars in multiple bank accounts and my living standards had not changed. So, what did I do? I went and bought a house. I bought a house. It was a BIG mistake. I shouldn't have done it. I got seduced into it. I thought I needed to have the house and I got trapped in that one location. I shouldn't have bought that house.

So, at this point, you should not be buying homes. You should not buy anything that does not spit more income back at you, even if it's a drip. A half of 1% from the bank on a million dollars is better than having a million dollars in a house. At this point, you have the money, but why? Really, WHY? Because you want to take that money and make your first real Wealth Scaling investment.

Back in the 1st Phase: Earned Income, what did I tell you to invest in? Only things that are within your 36-inch circle, right? Everything is close, within reach. You can touch and control it. Everything is symbiotic. Everything is parallel.

When you make your first investment in the Wealth Scaling phase, it's going to be something way out of reach — out of your 36-inch circle. So, you need a lot of those two things I mentioned: courage and money. I can't tell you what the investment number is for you. I don't know how lucky you are. Myself, I've never been a lucky guy. And I've never had a tremendous amount of courage. So, because I've never been lucky and because it feels like I have to work harder, I create this belief that I got to overwork the situation. I've always been extremely, extremely, extremely conservative.

Could I have done some things sooner? Maybe. But I know this, When I made my first investment, my first big Wealth Scaling investment, I used one third of my money. It was way outside my comfort zone because it wasn't in my 36-inch safety circle. I'll be talking about what it was in the next segment. I want to give you some ideas about things you could invest in.

STEP #8: INVEST (TO SCALE WEALTH)

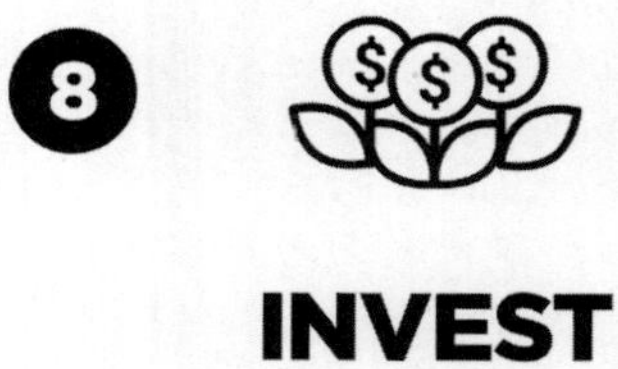

When I reached this step on the Wealth Wheel, my first time around, I was basically looking at three investment options. First, the house I've already told you about. And like I said, that was stupid, ridiculous. I put $150,000 into a house. Boom, the money's gone. I don't even call it an investment. It was dead money. It sits there. I can't touch it. Can't get to it. What is the purpose of money? To create more money, not to buy a house. I should have rented the place.

I know someone is going to be writing to me asking something along the lines of, "Dude, is a house a bad deal?" Absolutely!

One of the worst things you could ever put money into is a single-family home.

The second investment was $50,000 that I gave to a guy. Scott Morgan, a partner that came to me, said, "Hey, I want to create a business with you that's an extension of the company you run right now. It's going to be symbiotic." You've heard me talk about this, a parallel company. I said, "Look Scott, I'll lend you $50K to start the company. You have to pay me back in 90 days when the business starts making money." I did. It did. He did. And that company has made me money for over 20 years now. That was the second investment. It was only $50K. It wasn't a big deal and I got paid back.

The third investment I made was the $350,000 investment I mentioned a bit earlier. It was an apartment deal, a 48-unit multiplex, so multiple flows, in Vista, California. I put $350,000 down on a deal that cost me almost 2 million. I had a loan of $1.6 million, the property paid.

The property was miles and miles away from good ol' Uncle Grant, in San Diego County. I made a long-distance investment in a piece of property for the first time. Why do I tell you all that? I'm not telling you that to brag. I'm actually telling you not to do this. Instead, start close to you. If you can't control a little bit of money, put it in a bank and make sure it stays there. Then, start controlling the income coming into you. If you can't control that, how are you going to control something a county or multiple state or country away?

At some point though, during your wealth creation journey, you reach a point where not every investment you make can be within "arms reach" or "walking distance". It's inevitable. And when you do reach that point, it all really comes down to two words: "clear" and "certain". Investments at this level can get really complex, so it's extremely important for you to make sure of one thing when you make a high-level investment. It's simple and you can wrap your head around. If you cannot understand it, if you're not 100% clear, you should not touch it.

When it comes to big deal investments there are basically three possibilities. One is a "big bang" – an explosion out the back end. That's short term. The other is a dividend – cash flow or an inflow because you made an investment. That's long term.

As an example of this, when I invest in real estate and get a hundred dollars a month, that would be considered a dividend on my $10,000. I earn $1,200 a year on that. So, there's the big bang or the dividend or, in some cases, a combo of both. And by the way, I'm always looking for the combo; if I can get it, I like to see a little nibble on my fishing line, which means a little income every month plus the chance to catch a big one!

When it comes to specific criteria when you make an investment, there are a couple. Number one, you need to be certain. It has to be a sure thing. It's not a "maybe" or a "possibly". You want an ironclad "sure thing". And then, number two, I need to be clear. I have to understand what it is and know what I'm doing.

Whatever it is needs to be simple. You should be able to easily explain to someone else what it is and how it works. If you're not clear about what it is and exactly how it works, and if you aren't certain it will win, you shouldn't do it. So that's the criteria. Know what you're doing – keep it simple. Be able to explain it to someone else. If you can't, if you can't explain the business to another, you don't understand it yourself.

Failure to understand an investment means you're gambling and you never want to bet. If you want to bet, go to a casino. Betting is how you become poor, "knowing" is how you become wealthy. But to do this, you need to be extremely disciplined through this process – extremely disciplined and extremely focused, so that you can be someone who says, "I'm going for a big play."

You want to be paid while you wait for the bang – short term, the bang, long term, the dividends. Look for the combo!

Someone once told me, “You, you want your cake and you want to eat it too.” I said, “Yes, I do. Why else would I have a cake if I don’t want to eat it too?” So, you can have everything, but you have to be patient and extremely disciplined.

And it’s really key that you remember the order of operations when looking at an investment. Dividends are the most important. That’s the long term. A big bang is second. It’s short term and not predictable. Plus, focusing on a big bang means you’re hoping to get lucky. And if you’re lucky, you can’t do it a second time. The wealth that I’m helping you create, you can do a second time, a third time, a fourth time, a fifth time. You can do it in a down market, an expansive explosive market in a terrible market, in a monster recession. You can make money in every cycle using this formula.

As long as you think about the long and short term and handle all the downside, the world could come to an end but you and your investment will still be standing there.

Those are the kind of investments you want. Will the apartment building that you live in right now still be here 10, 20, 30 years from now? I guarantee it’ll still be here; no technology, no app is going to replace the roof over your head. It’ll look different maybe, but over the years, that has not changed much. Technology is changing all the time.

You don’t need to be in a hurry that anybody who wants you to invest now, before you have enough money, does not have good intentions. They just want your money. Hold off and take the time. If you’re at $20K right now, okay, and you don’t have a quarter million, take time to accumulate. Build your first flow. Keep focused. Keep improving yourself.

Take it in increments, so that one day you can get this in surges. Discipline yourself. Set the money aside and wait till you hit your target. Here, $250K — no less than that. And while you’re doing that, save all the time and energy you’re using to start doing homework on what you’re thinking about investing in. Because when you make the next swing, it's going to be a sure thing. It's not like you're going up there with your eyes closed.

I hope you hit it out of the park. No, actually, when you make that next move, that money is going to be a for sure deal, a guaranteed deal.

STEP #9: INCREASE NUMBER OF FLOWS

The final part of this last chapter is about increasing the number of income flows. This step could be called "Increase the Flows and Number of Flows.", but there's only so much space on an info-graphic! The point is existing flows should not be ignored here. So, we want to both increase the flows we have and start to increase the number of flows.

This step is honestly only for people who want to become truly wealthy. I'm talking about ridiculous amounts of wealth, in every area of life and business. This is where the big players play. They're always trying to create more flows. Some people think that these people are "greedy". But the thing is, these are the people giving out all the money. These are the people buying the hospitals. These are the people building the bridges that get named after them. These people no longer really think as much about money as they do about legacy. This is the difference between a "kingdom" an "empire" and a "dynasty".

The rich and powerful build kingdoms. The wealthy create empires. The truly wealthy create dynasties and leave a legacy. You want your legacy to live on. And for your legacy to live on, it would need to be funded. So let's talk about the flows. Some say that it's seven or eight flows for the average millionaire, but I don't believe that. I would expect the average millionaire to have 12 to 15 flows. I know myself, I'm somewhere between 50 and 60 flows of income, depending on how you count them.

If you look at billionaires and billion-dollar companies, they have thousands and thousands of flows. For instance, any major grocery store has 50,000 to 60,000 flows of income in one location. So how do you get there? You need to start thinking about a minimum of a dozen flows of income. And to start with, take some time to think carefully about each flow.

At 25, I had one flow. It was called a job — a job I "hated". The second flow was another job in that same company, in the finance department. When I sold a car and then I financed it, I got paid on both transactions. The third flow I added was sending referrals. If I didn't have the car you wanted, I'd send a referral to one of my buddies and I'd collect a commission on that if they got you into one. The fourth flow was for me to start doing other things in other departments that generate revenue.

On top of that, there was my savings account and my checking account, which were paying me a tiny stream of income in the form of interest. So, I had six total income flows, two of which were very small.

Then, at 29 years old, I went backwards. I quit the job and started my own business. That took me down from 6 flows, back to one main flow (other than my checking and savings). So, at that point, I had three little flows coming in. I had to start all over, working for myself.

And that's a mistake a lot of people make when they get to this point. They start a company and they end up going backwards when they do. Not only did I drop to one flow, but I also started needing to pay people to do things. I had to pay for my office, for supplies, for insurance, all that crap.

That's the problem with starting a business. Remember, 80% millionaires become millionaires from their jobs. 80% of all millionaires last year worked for somebody else. Only 20% of millionaires went out on their own and hit that level...

So, 80% of the people who become millionaires work for somebody else. That means their office is paid for, their desk is paid for, most of their expenses; the advertising, the marketing, the insurance are taken care of. You're not having to take care of that. This is why "Job Hate" is a trap. It might suck, but you should figure out ways to produce income from inside your job.

Now, let me fast forward. At 35 years old, I had a couple of businesses and was no longer a car salesman. I was selling though. I started a business where I did seminars. That was my core product, but it was all just one income. I would go out to your company, I'd knock on your door. It took tremendous amounts of outflow to get attention, with the hopes of getting some income. Let me cut to the chase for you — monster failure rate!

For three years, I only made $30K a year. Then, in the fourth year, I figured it out. It took me longer than it should have. It shouldn't take you that long. By the way, I didn't have any help. I didn't have any videos. I didn't have content. I didn't have support. I didn't have a mentor. I didn't have a mastermind group every Tuesday, but I was committed.

Now, the second thing I did with this seminar business, once I figured out how to make it work, was sell tickets. It was a cash business. Once I got my ticket sales figured out, I started adding products. My first product was an audio product. Then we added a video product.

So, I had a ticket for $395, although I typically gave this away for around $195 to get people into the seats. That way I could offer a $300 product. Then, in the end, I would offer a smaller audience the $9,000 high-end video program.

I took my first flow within 36 inches of me, and I added some products. I didn't reach outside of my circle. I did that for about three years, when a guy came to me and we started the second business, which was a consulting business, it fed off of that company.

There's a saying that I use all the time. Nobody understands it but me, "I eat my own arm off." By the way, looking back, I realize I should have been much more voracious and much more aggressive in the cannibalization of my own company. My partner did not want to cannibalize the company and it probably cost me a hundred million dollars. I'll explain that in a second. What that means is, don't jump to starting a company in China, just because you figure out Nashville. Go close to your own neighborhood. Go with something that doesn't require any more energy or effort. Stay symbiotic.

Make sure your businesses feed one another, back and forth. I'll give you an example. Here at my company, right now, we're running a big ad on a program. We have a particular push for the program, and I'm like, "Hey, why aren't you advertising this program over here?" My team's answer is, "Because if we advertise that, we'll lose sales here." That makes perfect sense. But here's the problem. You're always competing with everything. Somebody else is advertising that. Somebody else is advertising that price point. So, when you're in a company, you want to keep pushing all your products as though you're competing against yourself. The reason for that is pretty simple: you want the messaging that feeds your flows going out all the time to get in front of people.

Case in point, my consulting business with my partner who didn't believe in eating his own arm off. What happened was we fed them leads, but they didn't feed leads back to us. Guess what happened? It's the same thing that will always happen in a scenario like that. Which company do you think is going to die? I'm feeding them leads, and they quit feeding me leads. There's only one company that dies in that scenario, the one that quits feeding the other. It will always die sooner or later because of the way it thinks in terms of scarcity.

My next flow was a speaking business in a specific industry that I was familiar with. Then we added the consulting business. Both of those companies had multiple flows of income. I found out that I was pretty good at speaking. I was doing five and six free speaking engagements every day, 300 days of the year. So, in any given year, I would do 1500 to 2000 presentations. You do anything 2000 times and you're going to get good at it!

So, I added a speaking gig. I started offering speaking-related things to people. This income got so good, by the way, we increased it to two flows, then three. We added products that we would sell at the back of the room. If you've been to one of my seminars, you've seen this.

The fourth thing I did was take all the money from my other flows and dump it into real estate. And when I say, "all the money", I'm talking about every penny. I'm talking about calling my mom up and announcing it to her. My mom was my best friend. She was always the person I would go to and say, "I'm gonna go do this deal. I'm starting my real estate business."

First thing I did was buy 48 units. Then I went and bought another 38 units. Then I realized that I was pretty good at it, so I bought 92 units. That's what happens when you jump that fear chasm and truly begin to build wealth. The next thing you know, you own something significant, like my 500-unit complex in San Diego, California. That was rent coming in from 500 separate tenants.

But hopefully you won't make the mistake a lot of people make when they're collecting $1,000 times 500 tenants, which is to go out and buy a Bentley or a Porsche or a big watch and a ritzy crib to show off. You'll be better to do what I did and bank the money. Be rich but act broke.

If you're smart, which you must be since you've read all the way through this book, you're ready to follow the The Wealth Creation Formula. You're going to build your wealth, by creating income, increasing it, setting it aside until you hit your target, then invest it and create more streams of income and repeat the process until you have enough to make your BIG PLAY. And you'll do all that as all the while, you're acting like you're broke, unless it serves you to build real wealth. Watch for big bang opportunities, but make SURE the dividends are there. You want monthly cash flow. You want that drip.

I grew up in Louisiana where it's always wet and green. If you go out in Louisiana and there's no rain all summer long (which hardly ever happens) how do you water your lawn? You start getting brown spots everywhere and you just want to soak it. But soaking is not going to help. You have to give it a little bit every day. Same thing with flowers. Same thing for a tree. A tree actually grabs moisture every second of the day from the environment. It doesn't need rain. It'll learn how to grow in the desert. It sucks freaking oxygen. That's what wealth is: the ability to survive in any environment.

And speaking of "surviving" in any environment, back in 2008, I had 500 apartments. And then the 2008 recession came. Nobody knew it was coming. The bank that I owed the money to went underwater. The speaking gigs, the audios, the videos, the consulting business got cut in half, virtually overnight. Literally, one day I was rocking and the next day my business got cut in half.

So, when you're following the formula and creating wealth, on the way out of the middle-class traps, if you ever wonder why you need to be sure to do all of the steps on the wheel, the answer is simple. By 2008, most of my buddies got whacked. They got completely knocked out. And they weren't the only ones. Most of America, hundreds of millions of people, lost 30% to 40% of their wealth. The had bought into the great hoax — the middle-class American dream! Those people naively believed that they were wealthy and stable. The reality was, they weren't, because they didn't have the income coming in.

But me, I didn't lose any of my properties — not one of them. Nearly everyone else lost everything, but I didn't lose anything. Why? Because people were paying me every month. They weren't paying me as much, but they were paying me every month for something that they needed, no matter what was going on with the economy.

There were time periods, between 2009 and 2012, where I couldn't buy anything. And there will be times when you're out of the game, where you can't invest anything. Some of your flows may get cut down or even completely cut off, through no fault of yours. That's why this final step on the wealth wheel is so important. You have to increase the number of income flows, but never abandon your existing flows. You want to continue to increase the existing flows if you can. That way you can build additional flows.

For me, one of those was GCTV, my digital network. That, and my online training project, are bigger today than my real estate company. And this is how you build wealth. But like I keep saying, you have to be disciplined. If I went into "splurge" mode and started blowing my income on Bentleys and big watches, I would never have been able to start GCTV. And if I went into "scarcity" mode and was too scared to open my mind to new partnership models or to "eat my own arm", GCTV would never be as big as it is right now.

Today my first company is collaborating with people who I would never have thought of collaborating with 20 years ago. We actually sell other people's products out of that company today. So, I don't have just three flows, I have probably 40 or 50 different flows out of that first company. We also have a product called Cardone University. It has tens of thousands of users. In addition to that, Cardone Capital has over $4 billion in assets under management and I have tens of thousands of people paying me every month.

And why is reaching this level and executing this step, in a disciplined way, so important? It's all about legacy. You and your wealth can continue past your time. You can continue to give money to your church, your community, your mom, your dad. You can go on vacations and take risks; get freed up to make investments. All that means you'll get to go for the BIG plays that nearly no one else has enough courage to make. This is how wealth works. If you're not ready to create these kinds of flows, your legacy will die.

For me, that's basically five companies today with thousands and thousands of people being helped every day. All that floats information back to us. Probably 50% of what we do today, maybe as much as 80%, we do for free! Sounds crazy, right — seven high-end E books; seven webcasts a year; free content all over the web. How can I do so much for free? How can I hire people to help me execute on it all? That's how you build your brand, by building trust because you create value. You have to be willing to flow outward.

By creating wealth, you build your brand. And how do you create REAL wealth... by building value, by touching the lives of as many people as you can on this planet. It might come in the form of money to you, or silver, or cows, or sheep, or food, or milk, or bread, or whatever! But the truth is, it's something you're giving people and they're giving something back to you. It's the flow of life.

Remember the definition "wealth creation" is bringing a lot of something valuable into existence by creating an abundance of anything valuable. I'm not doing a job here. This isn't work for me. This is what all the heavy hitters say. Did this not work? They never even talk about it being work. They come in, they might complain a bit, because we're all human, but the truth is — they're doing life.

Look at Steve Jobs, iTunes, iPods, iPads, Mac Computers, you know what he did in the world. He brought a tremendous amount of value into people's lives. He won't be remembered for how much money he made. He'll be remembered for the impact he had on society, on the lives of so many people.

The question is, what would you like to be remembered for? How many lives do you want to touch and change in positive ways? I can tell you this, if you're the best friend to three people, those three people will say "What a great person.", when you die. But, if you could be the best friend to three people, why not be the best friend to thousands of people, or millions of people? Why be limited about how good a person you are, how generous you are, or how much you helped.

As we're winding up this book that I've put so much time, energy and love into, I hope you realize one thing. This book is part of my legacy. I know what I've been sharing with you here will change your life if you're ready to do the work and let it! I hope you go through the whole process of developing your own Wealth Creation Formula. You don't deserve to stay stuck as part of the poor-poor or poor middle class.

I hope this last step in this final chapter and this whole way of thinking about escaping the middle-class trap and building wealth helps you. I would strongly encourage you to read this book a second time, a third time, a fourth time, a fifth time, a sixth time, to make sure you understand all the steps and levels I've covered.

Just to end things on a memorable beat, let me tell you why the octopus is my favorite animal. It's because the octopus is extremely powerful, intelligent AND it has eight arms. That means they can hold onto many things, so they can move. And so, they can do more. If you can do more, you can BE more. You can help more people. When you can do that, you can have more and you can take care of yourself. I hope this book finds you well. I hope this makes you better. Let me know how you're doing on your pathway of wealth creation, as you escape the middle-class trap.

CONCLUSION

HOW TO MAINTAIN WEALTH MOMENTUM

The reason I not only wrote this book, but also included your Wealth Creation Formula, is I feel like it's my job to motivate you to actually implement and execute the actions I know you need to take. Let's face it: The "man", the media and the misinformed are NOT going to help you escape the trap. They all benefit from keeping you stuck in the trap, so you're going to have to do it yourself.

Taking the time to pick up this book and read it tells me that you truly do want to do something to change your situation. I want to congratulate you for that. Good job on getting the book and reading it and even more for finishing it. Now, if you want things to really change, it's time to put the lessons in it to work.

I want you to tell a few people what you love about this book. A big part of wealth creation is helping others succeed. When people with common goals and motivations come together, they tend to learn faster and become a support system for one another. So, gather a group of like-minded, highly driven people who refuse to stay stuck in the middle-class trap!

Help each other apply and commit to following the Wealth Creation Formula—and hold one another accountable. You can even create a study group and go through one chapter per week in a discussion session. Teaching others and being part of a group will galvanize your understanding of the material. It will increase your need to perfect what you've learned and put it into action. It will also immediately connect you with other like-minded people who want to improve their futures, and it will extend your power base.

I'm guessing that you didn't pick up this book because you're comfortable or satisfied being stuck and left-behind. Chances are you want to improve your current position. The truth is that will require you to engage in actions outside your comfort zone.

I suggest that you become a living, breathing example of each of these principles and put them into consistent motion. Your financial life, personal confidence, and overall outlook all depend on the results you get. I have great hopes for you, and I encourage you to take the information inside this book and use it to make sure that YOU and YOUR ACTIONS — not the "man", the media or the misinformed — determine the financial future of you and the people you love.

AFTERWORD

Whether you're riding a wave of financial good fortune right now or in the middle of a downturn, the ideas and principles found here will have one of two effects. They will either advance the wave you are on or allow you to start creating wealth for yourself — while others become financial victims. Whatever the negative conditions in which you find yourself, the right actions — performed consistently — will help you along your way.

I don't want you to be one of those people just "getting by," constantly living in fear. I want you to create wealth, so you can stay independent of what is going on around you. This book should be used as a reference guide for you and your family to measure your progress. Whether you're trying to create greater levels of wealth or simply escape the middle-class trap, this book will show you how to do it!

Be careful not to misinterpret these tools because they may seem counter-intuitive... The most effective tools usually are. And don't just read this book one time; you will change with your experiences, and you will see new ways to use this material each time you read it.

While the rest of the world is preoccupied with problems, your job now is to fill your every thought and action with the solutions that will allow you to advance and escape! I am truly interested in the success you find from using this information, and I welcome your calls and emails.

Prepare yourself for a great adventure as you start creating wealth! And remember, this formula can just be repeated, over and over again. The cycle never ends. And there is no real limit to the amount of wealth you can create.

May the actions you take daily set a good example for those around you. Let others see that anything is possible when you have focus and the correct information — and when you take the right actions!